IN THIS NEW BOOK ON HUGGING YOU'LL LEARN—

- ☛ WHY HUGS ARE GOOD FOR YOUR HEALTH
- ☛ HOW WOMEN PREFER TO HUG
- ☛ WHY MEN LIKE DIFFERENT KINDS OF HUGS
- ☛ TIPS FOR BECOMING MORE HUGGABLE
- ☛ HUGGING SECRETS FROM THE ORIENT
- ☛ HOW TO DO MORE THAN 20 TYPES OF HUGS

Here's the latest guidebook by William Cane, world-famous author of *The Art of Kissing* and *The Book of Kisses*. Based on an Internet survey available to 20 million people worldwide, *The Art of Hugging* examines every aspect of friendly, romantic, and sexual hugging and is sure to bring you hours of intimate hugging fun and excitement.

Praise for William Cane's *The Art of Kissing*

➤ "Get it and expand *your* puckering portfolio."

—*Seventeen*

➤ "Whoever said 'a kiss is just a kiss' didn't get his mitts on *The Art of Kissing* . . . a detailed how-to book . . . this year's handy alternative to chocolates."

—*Elle*

➤ "I advise you to race full speed to your bookstore and pick up a copy of *The Art of Kissing* . . . it could save you emotional problems."

—*Clarion Ledger* (Jackson, Mississippi)

➤ "The definitive book" [on the subject of kissing].

—*Mail* (Oxford, England)

Also by William Cane

The Art of Kissing, completely revised
and updated edition

The Book of Kisses

The

Art of Hugging

William Cane

St. Martin's Griffin
New York

For my friend Rhea Becker

Library of Congress Cataloging-in-Publication Data

Cane, William.
    The art of hugging   /   William Cane.—1st St. Martin's Griffin ed.
      p.   cm.
    Includes index.
    ISBN 0-312-14096-7
    1. Hugging.   I. Title.
BF637.H83C36   1996   95-40764
394—dc20   CIP

First St. Martin's Griffin Edition: February 1996
10 9 8 7 6 5 4 3 2 1

Contents

PART THREE: HUGGING TECHNIQUE

$\mathcal{P}$REFACE

"You're *what?*"

"I'm marrying Jimmy."

"How *could* you?"

"I love him."

"But only last month you told me he drove you crazy. You said he's loud and brazen and arrogant and you were thinking of telling him it was over for good."

"Oh, I was just upset because we had a fight. But now everything is back to normal. I guess I never told you how terrific things can be when we're not fighting."

"Gosh, Laura, this better be good!"

"Well, when we were apart I really missed his hugs. He's a magician when it comes to touch. He hugs me for hours. It's like medicine being with him. I feel like I belong in his arms. When he hugs me I feel so happy! He's such a sweetheart."

That's all Laura told me during our phone conversation, but of course I wanted more details. When I lecture at colleges across the country on the subjects of kissing and hugging, I always talk with people after my presentation. They often tell me intimate details about their relationships. But primarily I have three women to thank for the insight they have given me into their lives. One, a wealthy lady in her late forties, was especially helpful in telling me about some members of her family. The second, a newspaper reporter in her midthirties, discreetly shared with me the secrets of her married life. And the third was my friend Laura, an extremely beautiful young woman who has had numerous romantic encounters and who often took the time to tell me the inside details of her love life, details that I was as eager to hear as you will, I hope, be eager to read. Naturally names have been changed to preserve everyone's anonymity.

In addition to these confidential sources, this book is based on a 246-question survey distributed via Usenet newsgroups and E-mail that was available to over 20 million people worldwide. We received responses from 1,269 men and women, ranging in age from thirteen to sixty-eight, in twenty-three countries.

The book contains plenty of practical advice on how to make yourself more huggable based on actual responses. It also examines more than twenty different types of hugs—from basic heart-to-heart and side-by-side hugs to more unusual moving hugs and group hugs and specialized forms of hugging such as holding hands and hugging in bed and during sex—explaining how to do every hug and highlighting what men and women like and dislike about each one. The final section on hugging technique is the result of tabulating and analyzing comments from people all over the world.

How can this book help you?

If you're a guy, this book will tell you what women want. You'll learn why they crave hugs and how hugging can make them love you more. Most important, you'll learn how to hug so that your lover will feel like she's melting in your arms.

If you're a woman, you'll learn why men think of hugs in a slightly different way. You'll learn how to talk with them about hugs and how to get your partner to hug you the way you like—especially if you give this book as a gift.

If you received this book as a gift, consider yourself lucky. Your friend, lover, or sweetheart thinks enough of you to believe you can share some new hugs together. I hope you enjoy the experience of reading it, and I hope you enjoy the hugs that will inevitably follow!

Acknowledgments

I'd like to thank Carla Mayer Glasser, my very creative literary agent, for giving me the idea for this book. I'm indebted to the librarians at Boston College and the Boston Public Library for their expert assistance. The office of information technology at Boston College provided invaluable technical support for the Internet and World-Wide Web part of the research.

Last, but certainly not least, a big thank you to the men and women who revealed their secret feelings about every aspect of hugging by answering our rather comprehensive survey.

PART ONE

The Hugging State of Mind

WHAT IS A HUG?

I was in the office of a distinguished etymologist who teaches at a prestigious university in Boston. An etymologist is an expert on the origin of words. I was waiting for him to answer my question about the origin of the word *hug.*

"Sounds like a sort of caveman word doesn't it?" he said. "But I better look it up."

He took some dictionaries off a shelf behind his desk and after a few minutes of cross-checking he had the answer.

"The verb *hug* apparently comes from the Old Norse verb *hugga,* which meant to comfort or soothe, as a mother hugging her child. The word *hug* is most likely echoic, which is to say that it developed from people imitating the natural sounds they heard during a hug! For example, from the accompanying words of comfort or sounds of lullaby."

What he said convinced me that the word *hug* is a playful word, and it's useful to realize that hugging isn't a dry academic subject! It is a living subject, changing every day as people put their arms around people they love and hug them.

Hugs are good for you, too.

What good are hugs?

Hugging has more benefits than you might at first expect. Research indicates that hugging helps people both psychologically and physically. In order to see how hugs benefit us, we must turn to lovers and scientists.

Scientists?

Believe it or not, there's an entire field of clinical psychology devoted to studying hugs. Even as you read this, doctors in white lab coats are conducting tests on hugging and tactile contact at major universities around the world.

In *Codependent No More: How to Stop Controlling Others and Start Caring for Yourself* (New York: Harper, 1987) Melody Beattie reports that in the 1970s researchers began studying chemicals called endorphins, found in the blood and nervous system. Endorphins are morphinelike substances that reduce pain and cause us to feel euphoric. Studies show that *these natural narcotics, produced by the brain and nervous sytem, are increased when we hug.* When Laura told me her boyfriend's hugs were "like medicine" to her, she wasn't kidding. Physiologically, hugs are natural painkillers.

Leo Buscaglia has made a career out of telling people about the relationship-building value of hugging. He has done so much to foster the art of hugging that in *1001 Ways to Be Romantic* (Weymouth, MA: Casablanca Press, 1994), Gregory J. P. Godek points out that March 31—Leo Buscaglia's birthday—is Hug Day!

Other scientists have a lot to tell us about the value of hugs and tactile contact between humans. For instance, did you know that hugs can boost your immune system? This interesting fact is discussed by Ashley Montagu in his book *Touching: The Human Significance of the Skin* (New York: Columbia University Press, 1971). It seems that there is an area of the brain that develops in response to tactile stimuli. If a baby doesn't get hugged enough, part of its brain atrophies and its immune system suffers.

Hugs early in life make us capable of love. Infants raised without hugging tend to grow up incapable of loving others. They can become psychopaths, sociopaths, and pathological misfits.

Cross-cultural studies show this startling finding: Societies with less hugging tend to be more violent. Research conducted by neuropsychologist James W. Prescott strongly suggests that babies who aren't held and cared for are much more likely to grow up to be killers.

That's right. Killers.

Sidney Jourard, a psychologist interested in touch, discovered that Europeans touch more than Americans. He traveled throughout Europe watching people in restaurants and public places. As Helen Colton reports in *The Gift of Touch: How Physical Contact Improves Communication, Pleasure and Health* (New York: Seaview/Putnam, 1983), Jourard recorded how many times Europeans touched friends they were with. They touched on average one hundred times per hour, while Americans touched only two or three times per hour. A later chapter in this book will teach you a few things about how to touch and hug like a European. But for now let's leave these scientists and meet a few flesh-and-blood lovers who can give us another perspective on hugging.

What do you like most about hugging?

Men and women both like the warmth and sense of security that they get from a hug, but women's top reason for hugging is that it makes them feel loved. Men rated "feeling loved" fifth.

The greatest difference between the sexes when it

comes to hugging is that men like the feel of a woman's breasts, and women seem to be more sensitive to the emotional connection that comes with a hug. The following top ten lists are based on responses from 1,269 men and women and show what they like and dislike most about hugging.

Top ten reasons why men like to hug

1. It's warm
2. It gives me a sense of security.
3. It calms me down.
4. I feel like I have a real friend.
5. It makes me feel loved.
6. I can smell my lover.
7. I enjoy the sexual excitement I experience.
8. I like the feel of breasts.
9. It makes me feel I belong.
10. It's a chance to give and receive love.

One issue on the women's list doesn't appear on the men's list at all, number 10, "It makes me feel important." Interestingly, women placed more emphasis on feeling connected and close than on security. But both men and women rated "feeling secure" near the top of their lists.

What do people *dislike* about hugging?

Most people dislike it when someone *they* don't like hugs them. One woman says that when someone she doesn't like hugs her, she amuses herself by making funny faces over their shoulder. "After all, they can't see me so it's not

Top ten reasons why women like to hug

1. It makes me feel loved.
2. It makes me feel we're connected and close.
3. It gives me a sense of security.
4. It's psychological support, like therapy.
5. It's warm.
6. It lets me share emotions when I'm down—or up.
7. It makes me feel safe.
8. It's comforting and makes me feel cared for.
9. I like body contact.
10. It makes me feel important.

going to hurt their feelings. And, hey, if the hug isn't doing anything for me, I might as well do something that will keep me happy." Sometimes she can see herself doing this in a mirror and she has to stifle a laugh.

Many people also dislike hugging back someone who doesn't like them. This subject is treated at greater length in the chapter on the unrequited hug.

People also dislike courtesy hugs because they're not sincere. Says one woman, "I dislike it when I have a genuine desire to hug someone and they don't really hug me back."

Some women dislike when people misinterpret their intentions during a hug. Others dislike the awkwardness that can accompany a hug. "Sometimes people don't expect a hug, and you have to decide whether to hug or not," says one young woman.

About 25 percent of women dislike it when a guy starts pawing them during a hug. Here's some advice from a savvy sixteen-year-old on how to keep your hugs romantic: "Do not grab the girl's butt! It's demeaning, immature, and gross, especially if it's intended to be funny. It's *not*."

A few men dislike having to hug other men. Clearly they haven't studied the chapter on the same-sex hug.

A small percentage of guys dislike smelling the body odor of the person they hug. (More men, however, enjoy smelling their hugging partner.) About 2 percent of men get embarrassed when they hug a woman and feel the straps on the back of her bra. (Substantially more men enjoy the feel of the bra straps during a hug. There's more on this subject later in the book in the chapter on the sexual hug.) And about 30 percent of men say there's nothing they dislike about hugging. My advice for women? Try to find one of *these* guys.

What do you think about while hugging?

It seems to me that part of what a hug *is* must also include what you *feel* during the hug. Of course, there's really only one way to find out. "What goes through your mind while hugging?" I asked. Responses range from rather mindless things like, "*Mmmmmmmmmmm!* This feels great!" to some very complex and intricate mental processes.

Quite a few people are trying to figure out what *you're* thinking. In other words, they're wondering how *you* feel about *them*. As a young man says, "I'm wondering how much she's enjoying the hug." While hugging friends or close relatives, a thirty-year-old married woman from California says she thinks about how they are feeling and assesses their response to the hug. "If it's someone I'm hugging formally, I think about how long the hug should last."

Other people are concentrating on the physical sensations of the hug. A lot of men and women just focus on the feel of the hug itself. "Not much goes through my mind," says one twenty-two-year-old man. "I just sort of *exist*—it's almost a Zen thing." And an eighteen-year-old woman from Ottawa, Canada, says, "I'm not thinking about anything. My mind goes blank and my logic takes a rest. I can depend on the other person to take care of me."

Not surprisingly, many men get sexual thoughts during a hug. Although this puzzles some women and annoys others, keep in mind that the feel of a woman's breasts against a man's chest can be extremely stimulating, even if the woman is wearing a blouse and bra. About 25 percent of guys in their twenties think about a woman's breasts when hugging, especially if they can feel them against their chest. During a recent hug, one twenty-three-year-old fellow had these thoughts going through his mind: "I'm surprised she's hugging me. We hardly know each other. Gosh, she's got big breasts. I wonder if she's getting turned on, too? She smells like apples and cinnamon. I hope she does that again real soon."

Naturally, women can also have sexual thoughts during a hug, and many report that they do. But women seem more inclined to categorize hugs into three kinds: friendly, romantic, and sexual. Says one twenty-six-year-old woman from Sydney, Australia, "When I hug friends I'm thinking of projecting a friendly image. If I hug my boyfriend, I think loving thoughts. Sexual hugs are different, of course." These three kinds of hugs are treated in greater depth in later chapters.

Both women and men enjoy the feeling of bonding and closeness of a hug. One fellow from New Zealand says, "I enjoy having a primary need *to be needed* met." Women, however, more often than men mention experiencing specific emotions like love and closeness during a hug. A twenty-five-year-old married woman from Illinois says, "I usually think about the love I feel for the person I'm hugging or about the emotion I'm trying to convey (sympathy, for example)."

Hugs can mean different things to different people. They can mean different thing to *you* at different times. Surely women are on to something important when they tell us there are at least three different types of hugs—friendly, romantic, and sexual. Indeed, there were plenty of different answers to my questions about what you like most about hugs and what you think about while hugging. The bottom line is that hugs are what you make them. And the next chapter examines how men and women often experience hugs somewhat differently.

Sex Differences
in Hugging

"My boyfriend doesn't *know* how to hug!"

"I never get hugged the *way* I like."

"I'm never hugged enough!"

"Why doesn't someone write an instruction manual on how to hug?"

Typical complaints by women gathered from the first worldwide questionnaire on hugging conducted through the Internet. These comments strongly suggest that there is a need for an in-depth look at hugging that takes into account their point of view.

"She gets bent out of shape when I give her a squeeze in the wrong place."

"My girlfriend likes to hug too much."

"I like to hug but I also like to progress to other acts of intimacy, and she puts up roadblocks too often."

These comments from men gathered from the same survey indicate that there may be a sex-based difference in the way men and women perceive the subject of hugging. The responses from these men prompted me to examine the differences between men and women. I wanted to find out why men often feel that women like hugging for reasons that they do not understand.

Do men and women hug for different reasons?

Sometimes they do. Responses to the hugging survey show that while both men and women get pleasure from a hug, women often describe that pleasure in emotional terms, whereas men more often focus on the physical pleasure of hugging.

Diane, an extremely attractive young woman, is upset at her live-in boyfriend. She's argued with him every morning and every evening for the past week. When she goes to work she thinks about her problems and tells one of her coworkers what's going on at home. Her coworker is a handsome guy and a sensitive, good listener. He seems to understand. And one afternoon when they're alone in the office he gives her a hug to comfort her. An innocent little hug.

"It made me feel he accepted me. It also made me feel happy and loved. That's why I hugged him back. I had no intention of starting an affair. And I haven't started one— yet. But I am a bit worried about it. I don't know what may happen between us. But the reason I hugged him is simple in my mind. It felt good to have someone express an interest in me. Yeah, I guess you could call it love. Friendly love."

Diane hugged for the sake of companionship and love. She felt accepted and reassured when she hugged her coworker. This is often a key reason why women say they hug. "I enjoy the feeling of closeness," says a woman from Oregon. "It makes me feel loved" is a reason that appeared over and over in the survey responses.

Women tend to emphasize the emotional content of a hug. Perhaps they even interpret the physical sensation in a way that differs from men. While 41 percent of women mention the physical warmth of a hug as one of the pleasures of hugging, more than 92 percent of them say that the emotional component is the primary reason why they hug. For example, one young woman had been apart from her boyfriend, and when they got back together he hugged her. She says, "Recently my boyfriend came home from a three-week vacation. As we hugged, I really felt that he had truly missed me and was happy to see me and be with me again. It was as if he had new appreciation for me and his feelings for me."

For many women, the pleasures of hugging are centered on emotional comfort. A twenty-three-year-old married woman from California says, "Sometimes I just need a hug because I feel affection-deprived." A twenty-one-year-old woman from Oregon likes "the feeling of warmth from having another body close to mine, almost like having a live security blanket." Again the appreciation for the physical aspect of the hug is tempered by the observation that the hug has an emotional component—it provides security for her. A seventeen-year-old high school student summed it up: "While hugging, what goes through my mind is a feeling of warmth, not heat, but *emotional* warmth."

In contrast, 89 percent of the men sampled concentrate on the physical sensation of a hug. Although 63 percent also mentioned emotional benefits—such as feeling secure or loved—their main interest was the physical and tactile pleasures of the hug.

A thirty-year-old man says, "I hugged my girlfriend good-bye when she left for spring break. Afterward I thought, she's great, she's sexy, I'll miss her, can't wait to hug her hello." The sexual element is almost always there when a man hugs a woman. Nearly half of all men think about a woman's breasts when hugging, even if the hug is friendly or platonic.

In describing a recent hug, a thirty-one-year-old news-paper photographer said, "Earlier today a female friend/confidant from work was relating a story to a group of us in the news room. I was the only male present. Part of the story concerned a hug itself, and I quickly realized that my friend was going to use me as a prop to tell her story. She had never hugged me before. Just prior to the hug, I smiled because I was happy that she felt comfortable enough with me to give me a hug—and I was surprised that she was actually going to hug me. The hug was brief because, after all, its function was simply to demonstrate her story. I just had the briefest thought that I liked it anyway. Afterward I wondered about her physical attraction to me even though I know she is happily married."

A situation may be platonic, but thoughts of sex are never very far from a man's mind. It's no wonder that men sexualize hugs more than women do. The question that arises is whether men and women get into conflict over their different interpretations of the physical contact involved in a hug.

Do men and women have different expectations when they hug?

It depends on the kind of hug involved. Of the three basic types of hugs—platonic, romantic, and sexual—men and women have roughly similar expectations when it comes to platonic hugs. But they have slightly different expectations when it comes to romantic and sexual hugs.

Both sexes enjoy friendly or platonic hugs. While men may sexualize these hugs slightly more than women and may inadvertently get a sexual charge out of the hugs, they can and do accept the fact that certain hugs are platonic. Both sexes regularly enjoy platonic hugs with members of the opposite sex, and this subject is discussed in more detail in the chapter on the platonic hug.

In some ways men and women also see eye-to-eye regarding sexual hugs because both sexes report that they enjoy hugging before and during sex. But men and women differ when we discuss hugging *after* sex. Forty-two percent of women would like their husbands or lovers to hug them more after sex. For some reason, women have a greater need for hugging after sexual activity than men. "You should always hug after sex," says one woman in her early thirties. "It makes you feel better about yourself and makes you think that you mean more to him than just the sex."

Men and women also differ in their approach to romantic hugs. The greatest difference is that women often perceive a given hug as romantic whereas men see it as sexual. "I don't like being pawed during a hug" was a frequent complaint from both married and single women. Thirty-six percent of women dislike it when a man gets sexual during a hug when the woman's only intention is to be romantic.

Are women more aware of different types of hugs?

Yes. In general, women are more able than men to see gradations and shades of differences in types of hugs. Most men think of hugs in rather black-or-white terms. There are the short formal hugs you give your family, and then there are the hugs you get turned on by when you hug a woman. On the other hand, women can often distinguish between many different types of hugs and hugging situations. "Hugging a friend gives you a good feeling," one divorced woman wrote. "It's different from a romantic hug in that there's no agenda or plan to bring it further. Usually it's shorter, less intimate—depending on who it is, except with my daughter." In three sentences, this woman has differentiated between platonic, romantic, and family hugs.

What do women expect from men during a hug?

Women expect certain hugs to remain romantic, which means nonsexual. They expect that a man will hug them around the waist and give a little squeeze during a romantic hug. "Use eye contact and quiet talking, maybe soft hand movements," recommends one twenty-six-year-old. And a woman in her early thirties says, "Do little things like touch your partner's back and caress it gently, maybe touch her hair." Forty-two percent of women suggested that rubbing their backs would add some tenderness to a hug and make it more romantic.

"I don't like it when I'm in a purely romantic mood and he starts squeezing my butt or fondling me during a hug. It demeans me," says one forty-two-year-old woman.

What do men expect from women during a hug?

Men expect their girlfriends or wives to hug them with some passion. Many men have never learned to distinguish between romantic and sexual hugs, and they expect a woman to add some sexual elements to nearly every hug.

Some men also expect you to scratch their back during a hug. Others will be disappointed if you simply hug them without moving your hands. "The more she rubs my back and scratches it, the more interested I think she is," says a young man from Chicago. "If she just keeps her hands still I think something's wrong and I get worried."

How to make yourself more huggable

Simply wearing a bra will make you more huggable for over 80 percent of men aged eighteen to fifty. Seeing a woman whose breasts stick out excites a man and makes him want to get closer and hug. "Thinking about her breasts being pressed against my chest makes me want to hug her," says a thirty-year-old man who hugs his girlfriend from twelve to twenty times a week. Some men don't like the feel of a bra, but they are in a distant minority. Other men will get embarrassed if they feel your bra while hugging you, but they, too, are a minority.

What emotions make a man want to hug a woman?

Most emotions that bring people closer make you more huggable to the opposite sex. Says one young man, "Trust, affection, emotional intimacy, desire to communicate, happiness, grief, exhaustion—emotion in general makes me want to hug her."

Laura ran into a problem getting hugs from her boyfriend one summer when she began flirting with a salesman at work. Her boyfriend found out when he looked at their phone bill and saw all the collect calls the salesman had made to her. "That discovery put an end to any loving hugs for quite a while," she says. Once trust is broken, it takes time to heal the wounds. In the interim, hugs and kisses diminish.

Positive sharing of emotions can also make a man want to hug a woman. A twenty-five-year-old student says, "Celebrations of happiness make me want to hug. Of course, there are (unfortunately, it seems) many *serious* moments when I hug—to express my love, to convey warmth, compassion, and perhaps even a message that she is safe in my arms and welcome there at any time."

What makes a woman want to hug a man?

Women like to hug men who are sexy and romantic and who look like they can give a good hug in return. "I like to hug someone who has a firm, strong, yet gentle hug," says a twenty-three-year-old from Ontario. "If he has a nice body it makes me want to hug," says a twenty-six-year-old from New Zealand.

In addition to physical looks and build, women are inclined to hug men who seem needy. For example, more women said they would like to hug and kiss Woody Allen than Arnold Schwarzenegger. An accountant in her mid-twenties said, "If they seem like they need a hug, I will hug them."

How should men project a huggable image?

One way to project a huggable image is to keep in good shape physically. Thirty percent of women mentioned a strong body as a factor that makes them want to hug.

Men should also avoid being too thin or delicate. Women who had thin boyfriends often complained that hugging was "like hugging a skeleton." One woman said, "I feel like he's all skin and bones and it frightens me to hug him sometimes." And a twenty-four-year-old complained about her boyfriend: "I occasionally massage him but he doesn't like it much because he thinks I massage too hard. He is very frail and doesn't seem to be able to tolerate any pressure. I often wish he was stronger."

Most guys don't realize that they can also project a huggable image by being funny. "If a guy makes me laugh I'm more apt to want to hug him," says a college student. "If he has a sense of humor I feel more inclined to get closer and hug. Plus I like to laugh sometimes when I hug a guy, so that's important to me."

Another little-known fact is that, in general, taller men are more huggable than shorter men. "I like to hug tall, big guys, because they make me feel protected and safe," says one woman. Since it's impossible to increase your height once you've reached the age of about eighteen, the only thing you can do is wear boots or shoes that have big heels. "When he wears his work boots I love hugging and kissing him because he seems taller," says a high school girl from Texas. And one young woman from New Jersey says, "I sometimes ask him to stand on a phone book and hug him like that because it makes me feel like I'm hugging a giant. I don't know why, but I find that exciting."

How should women project a huggable image?

Men like to hug women who flirt with them. Teasing glances, perfume, a trendy dress, funky shoes—things like that heighten a man's interest. It's also important to be emotionally close. But beware of becoming too needy, which can be a turnoff.

Results of the hugging survey show that men don't like women who are overly dependent. Some jealousy and neediness is fine, but don't whine and complain to excess or a man is apt to shut down. It seems that a little independence goes a long way.

Is there anything you can do emotionally to make yourself more huggable?

Both men and women respond to a person who is emotionally available rather than one who is cold and distant. If you have a hard time expressing emotions (something that men have a problem with more than women) try to voice your feelings more often. Even expressing negative feelings can bring the two of you closer. Your partner will feel she understands you better, and this will lead to more intimate hugs. "I love it when he opens up with me," says a young woman who recently got married. "Even if he just tells me he's sad, it brings us closer together and I want to hold him to soothe him."

Next time you have a bad day and need to be comforted, tell your partner how you feel. You'll be surprised at how that little admission can lead to a hugging session in which you receive tender loving care in the form of caresses and hugs.

PART TWO

The Hugging Encyclopedia

The

$\mathcal{F}$IRST ROMANTIC HUG

Although some people are inclined to hug when romance blossoms and things heat up between them, most people kiss first. Sixty percent of men and 63 percent of women are more likely to kiss than hug on a first date.

But after that first kiss . . . hugs are just around the corner.

Two years ago Robin had an affair with a manager in the software company where she works, even though she was living with her boyfriend at the time. She saw the manager every day at the office and became good friends with him. When she learned he was going to be transferred to Texas, she realized how much she would miss him. They went out to lunch a few times, and then he invited her on a date. Her boyfriend worked the night shift, so it was relatively easy to slip out that one evening for a secret rendezvous.

"The first thing we did was kiss," she explains. "We were in his car overlooking Malibu Beach. The sun was going down and it was very romantic and exciting. Then we got out and kissed again. And then he put his arms around me and pulled me close. It was fabulous because I had been fantasizing about it for so long. There was also the danger of getting caught or being seen by someone who knew us.

I remember the way his arms surrounded me and how solid his chest felt. I have a rather flat chest, but it was still exciting to feel my breasts pressed against him. He was strong. I could feel his arms and hands, and it calmed me down and excited me at the same time. I don't know how else to describe it. I made love to him that night because it felt so good to be close to him."

First hugs aren't always so exciting.

A woman responded to the hugging survey with some details about hugging a friend at work who she liked. Their *first* hug wasn't too memorable, it just comforted her and made her feel good. But in the days and weeks that followed, her hugs with the coworker started to get longer and more intense. Her first hug simply paved the way for the exciting hugs that were to follow.

Most people don't have as many *first hug jitters* as they do first kiss jitters. This is because a first kiss usually precedes a first hug and prepares you for more intimacy.

How do you know if someone is ready for a first hug?

You can often size up someone's emotional need or readiness to be hugged by observing them carefully and talking with them. One woman in her early thirties said that she can usually tell if someone is ready for a hug by observing their behavior in an emotional situation. "I had a friend who left town last year, and although we were close we had never made physical contact. On his last day he took me out for lunch and afterward walked me to my car. As we stood by my car just looking at each other, I touched his arm, wondering how he would react. He took my hand and put his arms around me and held me tightly for a few minutes. Then he let go and said good-bye and walked away."

An eighteen-year-old said she sometimes can't tell and

so she asks when she thinks a hug would be appropriate. "If I don't know the person well enough, I often ask if they would be comfortable with me giving them a hug, and I add that I won't be offended if they say no." In her opinion it's always better to ask first rather than offend someone's sense of personal space.

What do you say to initiate a first hug?
Something *short* usually does the trick.

"Hug me."

"I need a hug."

"I want a hug."

"Give me a hug."

"I just bluntly say, 'Can I have a hug?' or 'Can I have a hug . . . please?' when I'm begging, or 'Gimme a hug!' when I'm feeling playful."

When you need a hug, do you have any nonverbal approach to getting it?
"Yes. I learned it from my fiancée. A really sorry, pouty look and outstretched arms. A hug is guaranteed!"

"Standing in front of her and raising my arms, beckoning with my hands."

"Just go up and open my arms out."

The
ℋEART-TO-HEART
HUG

A young mother and her toddler were playing at a party. The child was very affectionate, and every few minutes he would run up to his mother for a hug. But this kid had so much energy that he would climb up over her shoulder onto her back or clutch her leg or arm. She kept grabbing him under the arms and positioning him right in front of her. I watched this very carefully because I wanted to see how he hugged her. The fascinating thing was that he virtually ignored her breasts—he just reached out and put his hands around her, sometimes under her arms or around her neck, nuzzling his face into her shoulder-length hair. Her breasts were nothing special to him.

I have to admit I was actually jealous of that kid. Even her husband seemed jealous of his own son. He stood to the side, just eyeing them and scowling now and then.

But the kid's mother didn't pay attention to any of us, she just took care of her son. She seemed to have an intuitive sense that the most satisfying hug was the heart-to-heart hug. That's why she kept repositioning him onto her breasts so that they were chest-to-chest and heart-to-heart, cheek-to-cheek and face-to-face. She derived a lot of satisfaction from it—as you could tell just by looking at her smile.

And so did the kid, despite his squirming and climbing.

This hug is a classic, a hug to come back to again and again during any hugging encounter. If your boyfriend doesn't realize this, you may have to do what that mother did to her three-year-old, constantly repositioning your partner where you want him. Get him in front of you and hug heart-to-heart. "This hug makes me feel safe and secure," said one young woman. As another put it, "This kind of hug makes me feel warm and cuddly all over."

How to approach for a heart-to-heart hug

The first thing to keep in mind when doing the heart-to-heart hug is how to approach. Most people simply hold out their arms and walk toward their lover. "I have very open body language and hold my arms out, letting him know that I want to hug," says a young woman who hugs her boyfriend an average of ten times daily.

Some people have a more energetic method of approaching their lover and do it in a more playful way. Says one young man who loves hugging, "If I'm feeling particularly melodramatic, the hug approach involves coming up in a crouch with a huge open-mouthed grin and arms wider than Julie Andrews's on that mountain. Sometimes accompanied by a thoroughly nonmasculine squeal."

Occasionally the approach takes place from the side in a sort of flanking maneuver. One lover touches hips and then puts an arm about the other. Then both partners swing around so that they're face-to-face. A thirty-three-year-old box-office manager uses this approach frequently because of the special circumstances in which he works. "My wife and I both run the box office of a large theater in Washington, D.C. The space is so cramped that we usually can't pass behind each other too easily. I often bump into her side, and when the customer leaves I pull my wife close and then we turn face-to-face and hug and kiss. Sometimes I think we put on a better show in that box office than they do on stage!"

Benefits of heart-to-heart hugs

Most people find this hug relaxing. About 42 percent of people breathe slower during a heart-to-heart hug because it relaxes them so much. But says one young man, "Depending on the timing of the hug, sometimes I'm breathing faster and my heart is going Mach 3."

One of the chief advantages of the heart-to-heart position is that during it you can kiss your partner. "I love kissing during these hugs," says one young woman who recently got married. "He stands there and holds his arms around my waist and I lean back and look at him and then he pulls me close for a kiss. I love that feeling. It's like being on a swing together."

Twelve percent of women and 27 percent of men like this hug because during it they can feel their partner's backside. "It's convenient," says a woman who's dating a police officer. "We usually stick with the heart-to-heart hug because it's the most comfortable, and I can reach down and feel his butt." And a high school principal agrees, "I usually wrap my arms tightly around her, hands may just follow arms, or may caress her back, hair, bum."

Another benefit of this hug is that it's very romantic. The heart-to-heart position isolates the couple in their own little world. Said one woman, "I love the romantic feeling I get from this type of hug and the feelings of closeness, tenderness, caring, and sensitivity. It lasts as long as the moment calls for. I tend not to breathe during hugs if they are fairly short. If they are longer, like a minute or so, I probably breathe slower."

A final benefit of the heart-to-heart hug is that it's one of the easiest to do. Said one young fellow, "I guess this hug is nice because . . . well, you can't get it wrong. Ability to hug is innate, you know."

How do you break off from a hug?

WOMEN:
"I begin by pulling my head away, and the rest of the body follows."

"First I let go with my arms, then I move my body slowly away."

"I slowly let go of the embrace."

MEN:
"With guys, I've almost universally noticed the back-pat thing as a conclusion to a hug. Other than that, it's just how the moment feels. I'd say after about two seconds most hugs naturally come away, all the important things to be said being said."

"Relax the hold slightly and just slowly drift apart."

"Usually a slight release of pressure to see if it's reciprocated."

Drawbacks of heart-to-heart hugs

There are two main disadvantages to the heart-to-heart hug. The first is that when you're looking over your partner's shoulder you can't interact face-to-face. You can talk easily enough—because your mouth is close to your partner's ear—but you cannot see his or her facial expression unless you lean back and disengage partially from the hug. Says one young woman from South Africa, "You're really close to the other person. But it's not good in that you can't see him. So you're each looking over the other person's shoulder and that feels weird."

One way to avoid this disadvantage is to keep your faces touching—either nose-to-nose or nose-to-cheek. This kind of close interaction is one of the primary pleasures of the heart-to-heart hug. Says one young woman, "What I like best is the closeness, the contact, having our faces close."

The other drawback of the heart-to-heart position is that you may not know when to break off from the hug. Since this hug is very intimate—you usually have your arms around your partner and most of your body is pressed against theirs—people can get confused about how long the hug should continue. Says one woman, "It's difficult sometimes to read a person and how long the hug should last." Another woman feels that she can figure out how long hugs with women friends should last, but when it comes to hugging men she has more difficulty. Men have just as much difficulty knowing how long they should hug women. "If with a friend, I sometimes don't know how long is acceptable," says a forty-year-old political analyst.

One simple solution is to let the other person make the first move to break off from the hug. This way you don't have to think, you simply react.

When you hug standing up, where do you generally put your head?

WOMEN:
"I tend to put my head on my partner's shoulder."

"My head is usually to the side of the other person's head, ear-to-ear you might say, but not touching unless it is someone I know intimately."

"Next to his, like I'm looking over his shoulder."

"I rest it on his chest near his shoulder."

"I'm short, so that's an easy one—on the guy's chest, if it's a guy. If it's a woman, off to the side somewhere."

MEN:
"I never knew till you asked that I'm a to-the-left hugger— that is, I rest my chin on her right shoulder. Interesting!"

"I almost always try to put it cheek-to-cheek. I love that position. I can smell her perfume, feel the warmth of her face, and whisper in her ear."

"With my lover I tend to take the lazy man's way out. I usually rest it on her shoulder."

The
SIDE-BY-SIDE HUG

A young woman from New Orleans once sat beside me on an airplane. When she learned I was interested in the subject of hugs, she told me that she grew up in a very strict family that didn't hug much. "We hardly ever touched one another," she said. "So when I started dating I never hugged my boyfriend."

"And do you still refrain from hugging?"

"Oh, no." She laughed.

"What changed things for you?"

One afternoon she was walking with him along the wooden promenade of a levee that parallels the Mississippi. He happened to have a camera with him and suggested they take a few time-exposure pictures of themselves down by the water. They set up the camera on the boardwalk and then climbed down on the rocks that led to the river. While she was hurrying to get into position before the camera went off, she tripped and fell, twisting her foot between two boulders. The camera clicked and caught her sitting on the rocks. When she finally got back onto the boardwalk with Brad, her ankle was in pain. She had sprained it severely and had to limp back along the promenade with him helping her every step of the way.

"He had his arm around my waist and our hips were pressed together. I had my arm around his neck. I was in so much pain that I didn't think about what I was doing. Every few yards we had to stop. And when we stopped we just stood there in the sun, leaning against each other, hip-to-hip and side-to-side. People passed by and smiled at us. They thought we were lovers enjoying a moment of peace together. Little did they know I was suffering."

By the time they got to Decatur Street to take a cab, a full hour had passed. "During that hour I learned something about hugging that I never forgot. I discovered what a pleasure it is to be in contact with someone you love, even if it is just side by side. In fact, when we stopped in front of the steamboat *Natchez,* we asked someone to take our picture like that. I still have it. It shows us standing with our arms around each other in that side-by-side hug. Whenever we want to reminisce about the day our relationship started to get serious, we walk somewhere side by side. It's a cute way for us to remember how I broke out of a childhood of hug deprivation."

Her experience with the side-by-side hug only scratches the surface of a hug that's right for just about any situation from intimate to public. The best thing about this hug, according to survey responses, is the subtle interplay between your hip and your partner's. "I like the way his hip feels when we're walking together," said one young woman. "Once I even told him I wished we were connected at the hip so we could walk like this all the time."

Do you like to hug side by side? If so, where do you like to do it?

MEN:
"I always sit next to my fiancée at restaurants—even when it's just us two at a booth. It makes more sense because it

puts us closer together. A waitress once commented on it, she thought it was great (servers at this restaurant always joke that we're 'so cute' we brighten the whole restaurant—I'm sure they mean mostly my beautiful fiancée). We hug, snuggle, rest our heads on each other's shoulders, stroke arms and legs, and kiss. There's no better way to enjoy a meal!"

"I like to hug side by side in the weirdest places. We did it in class together when we were dating in college, sitting in the back of the room so that no one noticed. Now we do it when we're in the car. She sits next to me and hugs me while I drive. Sometimes we do it in a bank while we're on line together."

WOMEN:
"I love hugging side by side. It makes me know he cares for me. We hug like that when we're at parties. He stands there and I sort of lean up against him while he puts his arm around my shoulder and I put mine around his waist. When guests come up to us, we chat with them as a couple and they never think twice about the fact that we're hugging. It's a sort of sneaky hug because a lot of people don't even realize that your sides are in contact."

"I work with my husband in a hairdressing salon, and the chairs are close together. So we stand and hug side by side occasionally when we're cutting hair. Sometimes only the bottoms of our legs are touching or just our hips. It's fun to work and stay connected. I feel like I'm putting one over on the customers—they never even notice!"

How to do a side-by-side hug

1. Put your arm around your lover's shoulder.
2. Press your hip to your partner's.
3. Try to ensure that your thighs and lower legs are touching, too.
4. The hug can be accomplished while walking slowly. Note that the more forcefully your hips and legs are pressed together the slower you'll have to walk.
5. Side-by-side hugs are also possible when lying down or sitting.

According to survey replies, this hug is very popular in Europe, especially in Italy and Greece, where many respondents hug side by side while strolling along a beach or shopping on a crowded street.

The
ℬACK-TO-FRONT HUG

Leanne has a problem. Her husband likes sports so much that he watches a basketball game on their wedding night. Before their honeymoon he calls ahead to make sure the hotel has ESPN. She can't seem to get him to change. He spends far too much time watching television, and *he* doesn't think it's a problem.

On their honeymoon cruise he sits in their cabin with a pillow propped behind him watching a hockey game. That's when it occurs to Leanne that she misses contact with him so much she might as well try something new.

So she crawls into bed in front of him.

"Hey, Lee! I can't see the game!"

She ducks down and moves to the side, wriggling to get between him and the television. He squirms this way and that to see the screen.

"What are you doing?"

"I want to be with you, Derrick."

She sits in front of him, her feet stretched out on the bed, her back to his chest, his outstretched legs on either side of her thighs. His head is right behind hers, but if he moves two inches to the left he can see the television just fine.

"Now we can watch it together," she says.

He doesn't say anything at first. Eventually he puts his arms around her waist and she snuggles back into his embrace.

"I love sitting like this," she murmurs.

When the commercial comes on she cranes her head around and smiles at him.

Seeing as how it's a commercial, he kisses her.

Night after night this is their compromise. By the time they get to Aruba it's second nature to them. She likes it and strangely enough so does he. In fact, 70 percent of women say this is one of their favorite hugging positions. While 25 percent of women prefer sitting or standing *behind* the man, and 5 percent don't care either way, most women like the man behind *them,* the way Derrick sits with his back against the cabin wall (maybe with a pillow or two behind him) with Leanne sitting in front of him and snuggling into his chest, holding his arms tight around her.

Fifty percent of men also prefer being behind the woman. Only 25 percent prefer having the woman behind them, and 25 percent don't care whether they're in front or back.

This back-to-front hug is perfect for private as well as public places. As one young man explained, "I love how I can nuzzle her neck and smell her hair or kiss her ears and shoulders. While waiting in line or looking at something, it's more intimate than side by side. We can whisper to each other what we're thinking."

Although most women like it when the man is behind them, they also occasionally like having the opportunity to stand behind him when he's doing some chore. Leanne usually finds it easier to sit in front of Derrick when they're watching television, but there are plenty of other times when she likes hugging *him* from behind. "Now that we're married I hug like this all the time in bed or if he's cooking or washing dishes and he can't or doesn't feel like turning around. I love the feel of my breasts up against his back, bare or clothed. This type of hug can be especially intimate."

Interestingly, many people enjoy this hug in public because it identifies them as a couple and they want the world to know they're with each other. "In public," says one married woman, "I stand behind him and hug him sometimes because it's another way of identifying that we're together. In private, of course, it can lead to more sexual things."

A curious fact noted by anthropologists is that when a man and woman have to pass each other in a crowded situation, such as a packed bus or subway car, the man usually squeezes past the woman with *his front toward her,* while she usually squeezes by with *her back toward him.* Maybe this accounts for the reason that most women prefer having the man behind them in a hug like this.

When women do find an opportunity to hug their man from behind, they often get a little thrill out of the power reversal that seems to occur. A seventeen-year-old noticed this: "I very much enjoy this type of hug. I feel like I'm in control because I'm the one putting my arms around *him* and I have the greater advantage of kissing, changing position, and talking. I also do it when I know that I'm more affectionate than he is by nature, since he really doesn't have to do much except stand or sit there. Besides, I'm aggressive in general about romance, usually more so than my boyfriends."

Most men feel protected when a woman hugs them from behind. It's a kind of maternal warmth and protectiveness that one twenty-year-old engaged man mentioned. "I love having her hug me from behind with her chest to my back. It makes me feel protected, safe, cared for. I like the feeling of her body (and respective soft parts) against my back."

A sexual variation on the basic back-to-front hug

One of the most common sexual variations of the back-to-front hug can occur only when the man is behind the woman. In this position he can raise his hands up to her breasts. A good example of this hug occurs in François Truffaut's film *The 400 Blows*. Many men and women enjoy this type of sexual element in the hug. "It's fantastic, very sensual," says one fellow. "She bends back and kisses my chin, or I kiss her forehead. Sometimes these hugs are so intense I feel like I'm in a Calvin Klein commercial."

When your lover hugs you from behind, does he ever raise his hands to your breasts? Do you like this type of hug?

"I like it when he does this, especially if his hands are warm (which they usually are) because I'm always cold—sometimes so much so that my nipples ache—and his hands take that sensitivity away."

"He does, and it usually annoys me."

"I don't particularly enjoy this because I feel that it sexualizes the hug, and I prefer to feel more cuddly when I hug."

"Yes, he does this all the time. I used to think it was weird, but now I've gotten used to it and I like it. If he doesn't do it, I get upset. Usually this is when we're getting ready to go to bed and are already lying down."

"This is a very sensual way to hug and I find it extremely arousing."

Let's get back to the tender and nonsexual side of this hug for a moment. Probably the nicest thing about a back-to-front hug is that it can be done in public. And the most *subtle* variation of this one hardly even involves the hands at all. It's more of a *quiet standing* behind your partner. Get close, close enough to feel her body heat and smell her perfume. Gently put one hand around her waist—lightly, so lightly that she doesn't even notice it's there. Trust me, she knows *you're* there. She loves the fact that you're there beside her, behind her, close by. Just standing there like that now and then—maybe when you're on line waiting to see a movie—that subtle connection is the essence of romance. You're expressing your feelings for her simply by being there. Now what more could you ask from a hug?

The

$\mathcal{C}$OMFORTING HUG

I got out of the Ford at the top of the hill and looked down at the procession of limousines crawling through the fog. It was too early for me. I hadn't even had breakfast yet. I was wishing I had at least a cup of coffee in me. You could say I was in a sour mood. I hate mornings, funerals, and grave-yards.

I didn't even know the dead man that well. His name was Roland, and he had been a member of my college fra-ternity. The whole thing was more like a college reunion and it was starting to get on my nerves.

Roland's brother got out of the limo two cars back and started walking toward me. His name was Huey and I felt guilty because I didn't want to talk to him. He was a bit overweight, and his black suit jacket looked like it was going to burst at the seams. He had a doughnut in one hand and a Styrofoam cup in the other. You could hear him huffing and puffing as he got closer.

"Hey, I haven't seen you in years," he said. He took a deep breath and stuffed the remains of the doughnut into his mouth. Then he handed the cup to the funeral director and put his arms out to hug me.

It seemed to be happening in slow motion. I didn't want

to hug him. I had never really liked him or his brother. I was here only out of loyalty to the fraternity. But when he reached out his arms I could see that his eyes were red. It occurred to me that he had been crying. And then I could smell the coffee on his breath and his arms were around me and he was clapping me on the back and I was clapping him on the back and saying, "You old rascal, how the heck are you? We're all going to miss your brother's dart game."

Then he stepped back and grabbed my shoulders and gave me a smile. And I felt better after that. It was as if I had crossed a bridge. For some reason it hadn't been such a bad experience to hug him after all. It seemed to make him feel better, and I was surprised to notice that I felt brighter myself. Then the funeral director gave him back his cup and we began walking through the cemetery together.

Huey and I had shared that special type of comforting hug whose purpose is to console someone who has lost a loved one. It's a hug through which you can offer emotional support and express sympathy and condolences. Says one young woman about this hug, "All the bereavement hugs I've ever given or received involved a swaying or rocking motion. It seems to come naturally, and somehow the rocking conveys the special message of grief and sympathy and suffering felt by both hugger and huggee. Also, I've noticed that the bereavement hug lasts longer than most other hugs."

Comforting hugs are not restricted to funerals, however. They are appropriate in any emotional situation when a friend or family member needs reassurance. As one woman put it, "In an emotional situation a hug can be very reaffirming and help to give strength." Another woman gives comforting hugs in emotional situations "when the person needs a hug to stabilize them and calm them down." A nineteen-year-old from California, who doesn't hug often, says she'll give someone a hug only if she *or* the other person needs it in an emotional situation or after a long separation. Although she doesn't usually like hugs, she finds that in emotional situations they tend to calm her.

Like Huey, we've all known times when we were distressed, times when things were extremely difficult. And in circumstances like these nothing helps like a good hug from a friend—or even just an acquaintance.

"I had been injured and felt sort of neglected by my husband in the hugging department," explains a twenty-one-year-old woman from San Diego. "I felt as though he was scared I was too fragile to be hugged, yet my need for hugs had not changed throughout my recuperation period. I thought it was funny that my mother had not hesitated to hug me—in fact, she demanded it! After he finally hugged me I was much happier and felt closer to him. All of this was so much in my thoughts that I even told him this later."

When you're down and someone hugs you, it can really feel like charity.

"I had just gotten back from the computer lab," writes a student from Oregon. "I had spent an extra hour working on my paper because the computer crashed, and I was feeling pretty horrible. I went to my boyfriend's house and went straight into his arms for a comforting hug. While he was hugging me, I thought about how nice it was to finally be out of the lab and into the arms of someone who loved and cared for me and how snugly his arms felt. When we were done hugging, we cuddled for a while until I got my confidence back up and was feeling better."

Keep in mind that the person giving you a comforting hug may be very affected by your depressed mood. Be kind to them after they are kind to you.

Has anyone ever hugged you to make you feel better? Who?
Did it work?

MEN:

"I had a tiring week and saw my girlfriend on the weekend. We did a lot of stuff, including hugging. I was really tired. Sunday night I was writing in my diabetic logbook. My blood sugars were up and down more than usual. I started to question why they went up and down. Slowly I began to realize what I should have done compared to what I actually did. I forgot to buy one type of insulin and ran short of it. So now I had to compensate for forgetting and not having that type by using my quick-acting, short-lasting type. I was mentally beating myself up. I explained my frustration to my girlfriend. I was lying on the floor telling her and was feeling distraught, and she knelt beside me and put her forearms and hands on my chest and placed the side of her head on my chest and cried and told me she didn't know how to help me. I told her that just being there was enough."

"Once my lover held me while I cried about another woman who had broken my heart. She hugged me for about half an hour and made me feel better."

WOMEN:

"Yes, I have been hugged to be comforted when I was upset. And yes, it did help to have the hug. It's a very secure feeling when you're not having a good time of it. My husband held me tight and talked soothingly to me when I was really upset and having an anxiety attack."

"My friend and I have a signal for each other (mainly for me). When one of us is having a bad day and needs a hug, we say 'I need five minutes.' This tells the other one we need a hug, but no one else knows what it means."

How to give a comforting hug

Believe it or not, some people like hugging so much they go around seeking out unfortunate people who need hugs. They're almost like hug police. If they can ferret out someone who needs a hug and give that person a hug, they feel better themselves.

They start by having emotional antennae. Somehow they've sensitized themselves to the emotional needs of others. Usually it's women who have this talent. But, guys, if you're able to do this with your girlfriend or lover, she'll think you're a truly sensitive fellow. What these people do is try to find out how the other person feels. They actually put themselves in the other person's shoes emotionally.

One of the survey questions I asked was "Do you ever size up someone's emotional need or readiness to be hugged?"

"Yes, I do this all the time," says a young woman who's a senior in college. "When my friends tell me about something that happened to them that was traumatic, and they look like they need to be hugged to feel better or to cry and let it all out, then I hug them. For example, when my friend Paula was having problems with her friend Jeff, she sat with me and told me everything that had happened and how that made her feel. Then she started to cry. I could tell she wanted to be comforted, so I leaned over and gave her a nice long hug so she could cry and let me soothe her and tell her things were going to get better."

Once you've established that someone is in emotional need, your next step is to give a comforting hug. It's called a comforting hug because it's intended primarily to help another person rather than to share mutual joy or foster romance. And the comforting hug is relatively easy to do. This is usually because a person in emotional distress is so desperate that they'll appreciate virtually any kind of human contact. You can't go too far wrong technically in giving a comforting hug. And you may find that you get a boost from it, too.

As a young fellow from New Jersey explains, "I've given comforting hugs during funerals. And I was glad to do it." Why was he glad? Well, it may sound selfish, but it simply made him feel good to help someone else.

Another young fellow who's tall and built like a football player finds that women love to hug him. He explained how one day he was in a position to help one of his women friends with a hug. "My friend Cheryl was getting married and was very stressed during the rehearsal. Having coordinated most of the event herself, she bore a lot of the responsibility, not to mention added pressure from all the family stuff that sometimes surrounds these events. So, when there was a lull in the activities, I sidled up to her and quietly said, 'You look like you could use a hug.' She quietly replied, 'I was hoping you'd notice.' And we hugged. For quite some time. Our breathing synchronized and I could tell her stress was slowly dissipating. Sniffles from over my shoulder told me (as I later verified) that tears of relief were welling up. I told her I loved her and that I thought everything was going wonderfully. Through that hug I gave her my confidence that all would be well for her. And the wedding was beautiful and occurred without a flaw."

Those comforting angels

A great number of exceptionally attractive women are really charitable angels whose beauty is truly more than skin deep. For instance, one popular twenty-one-year-old from Idaho says that at the end of a date men usually want a hug. She gives them one even if she doesn't want one herself. That's charity!

One man from New York called an old flame when he was recuperating from a ski accident. She was going out with another guy but came over to visit him anyway. "She stayed quite a while. In fact, she gave me some of the nicest hugs I can remember. She felt sorry for me because my leg was still in a cast. She made me dinner and then we cuddled on the couch in front of the fireplace. I felt like she was a nurse sent over by the Salvation Army."

Angels of mercy.

Be on the watch for them. And hope they'll be there when you need a hug.

Have you ever given a comforting hug (where you know the other person needs a hug more than you do)?

WOMEN:
"Yes, on numerous occasions. Whenever my friends have a little breakdown and they look like they could use a hug, I give it to them. It always makes me feel like I want to do more, help, whatever, but this is sometimes all I can do. Often a person needs to be held to let his or her problems out."

"Yes, I've done this. I was listening to a friend tell me about his divorce, and he stopped talking and looked down like he was upset. I reached over and just put my hand on his arm, and he looked up at me. I didn't want to hold him if he didn't want me to, but I thought maybe he could use some contact. He reached out his arm and we hugged for a long time without talking."

"I produced a video documentary on survivors of incest, and the woman being interviewed had just told us her story. It was an extremely difficult topic for her to discuss, and she was visibly shaken. I wanted her to know that she wasn't alone and that she had support. I offered her a hug and she accepted, and I think we both felt better afterward."

"Yes, I have given a hug to make people feel better when they were upset, sad, and depressed. It's a way to comfort your friends and let them know that you're really there to help them if they need it, unlike when you just *tell* them you're there for them. Sometimes that isn't quite enough. The hug is a tender, gentle hug, but firm."

Male angels

Men can be angels of mercy, too, dispensing comforting hugs to men or women as needed. A young man from Georgia said he hugs friends when they're feeling blue. "It lets them know they're not alone, and that in itself usually makes them feel a little bit better."

Another fellow is often approached by people in trouble because of his friendly demeanor. In his opinion there are two necessities to cheer a friend who's sad or sick. "Miso (Japanese) soup and a hug. I give them all the time; I'm inspired to out of empathy, I guess. They're special—almost like you're asking friends to share their worries or weakness with you so you can deal with them together. The most deeply moving hug I ever got was saying good-bye to a friend in his hospital room. It was a hug that somehow seemed to pass a part of his spirit to me to keep after he was gone. It still stirs me today."

The
$\mathcal{G}$ OOD-BYE HUG

Midnight. Your boyfriend drops you off at home. He gives you a quick kiss. And then it starts—this worry. Sometimes your evenings out end with a knotty feeling in your stomach. You danced, you drank, you sang, you looked into his eyes and listened to him say sweet things to you. So why this anxiety when he walks away and you're on your own?

"I can't stand it if a date ends without a hug," says a high school student. "I like my boyfriend to hug and kiss me because it's the last impression he leaves me with for the night. I want to have that as a pleasant reminder of the good times we had and the good times we *will* have when we get together again."

Beginnings and endings are the most stress-filled times in any relationship. Smooth over those rough spots. Pay attention especially to the most difficult time of all, saying good-bye and good night. You'll feel better if you hug. You'll sleep better, too.

"There are two things I need at the end of a date," says a college student. "I like my boyfriend to say he loves me and I like him to give me a good-bye hug. It relaxes me and gives me pleasant dreams."

Seventy-five percent of men and women hug good-bye

near the end of at least *some* of their dates. Ten percent say they "always" hug good night at the end of a date.

Good-bye hugs are also great in the morning. When a couple starts living together, good-bye hugs often become the most meaningful thing they do at the start of their day. "It's a way of saying that we still care about each other as we're parting in the morning," says one young woman. "We say it without words every time we hug good-bye."

"It's a self-affirming type of hug," says another woman. "It makes me feel good all day. It's the perfect send-off when we have to part because it reminds me that there's someone who cares. It also reaffirms the fact that we're still a couple, and that's comforting, too."

The bedtime variation

The chief variant of the good-bye hug is the one many lovers give each other before bed. If your partner is going to sleep before you, this bedtime hug can be done outside the bedroom. Or it can be done in the bed itself as both of you drift into slumber. A twenty-four-year-old woman explained, "I hug my lover good night every night, generally for one minute to much longer, like when we're ready to fall asleep and need to get more comfortable." And a thirty-year-old divorced man from Ontario agreed with the concept of the bedtime hug as almost a security measure during the night. "When I have a lover to sleep with, I like to hug her all night, or at least maintain body contact in bed."

A young woman from Australia said that she hugs her lover "until we fall asleep if we're sharing a bed. Other than that, I hug him at night for maybe twenty seconds or so." This comment illustrates that a good-night hug need not be protracted in order to work its magic, making two lovers realize that they're a unit. Nevertheless, bedtime hugs often last much longer than daytime hugs. As one young man explained, "Do I hug my lover good night? Definitely—a hug and kiss before bed, always. And sometimes they last all night (we pass out like that)."

How to improve your good-bye hug

- ☞ When you're about to say good-bye, pause and look directly at your partner.

- ☞ Scrutinize your lover to see whether her lipstick is on right and she's got both earrings in place. Check that his tie is straight. They'll appreciate this helpful consideration even if they don't know what you're up to.

- ☞ Murmur a complimentary phrase like "Gosh, you look great! I'm jealous thinking of all those women you're going to be attracting today!"

- ☞ Groom your partner if you can. Fix his hair, adjust the lapel of her coat.

- ☞ Step up those final few inches and put your arms around your lover for a good-bye hug.

- ☞ If you're in a rush, hug quickly. (A short hug is better than no hug at all.) But if you can dally, by all means take the time to tell your honey, with the hug itself, how much you'll miss her when you're apart.

- ☞ Give an extratight squeeze midhug to say you're sorry to see each other go.

The
℘LATONIC HUG

If you're an adventurous soul, this has to be the most romantic type of hug there is. To some people, though, it's the most reckless and frightening. And all because you're hugging someone who's *not* your lover.

What's so dangerous about that?

Plenty—if you fail to make sure the hug remains a purely *friendly* encounter. People get into trouble all the time with this one. They start off innocently enough, but then things move ever so slowly in a risky direction. There's no telling what might happen when you start hugging friends of the opposite sex. Which is why it's important to understand the implications of this hug at the outset.

Our investigation into the platonic hug starts with Nellie, a twenty-six-year-old reporter from New Zealand. She's been arguing with her partner recently about his lack of attention. At work she broods about her problems and wishes she could talk with someone about them. So when the opportunity arises she confides in Doug, a male coworker she likes. She starts telling him about her difficulties at home with her lover. *And this is exactly where things can get dangerous.*

You could easily find yourself on slippery ground when you tell a platonic friend about your emotional or sexual problems at home. According to research conducted by Baltimore psychologists Shirley P. Glass and Thomas L. Wright, talking about problems can lead to emotional intimacy with your friend, which may in turn lead to sexual contact. In recent articles published in *The Journal of Sex Research* and the *Journal of Marriage and the Family,* Glass and Wright point out that women tend to have extramarital affairs only after they become emotionally involved with someone. The first step toward that emotional involvement is usually confiding in a platonic friend about problems they're experiencing at home.

In Nellie's case, things started off innocently enough. All she did was talk with Doug at work. But then one day he hugged her to make her feel better and comfort her. "And it definitely worked," she says. It was only a platonic hug, but she admits that she was also physically attracted to him. Over the next few weeks the hugs started getting longer— thirty seconds to a minute in length. She knew that something more might be developing and, frankly, she was worried about it.

So when is a hug *just* a hug?

I asked her what the hugs were like with her friend at work. Her reply contains one of the keys to keeping a hug platonic.

"These hugs are nice," she said, "but *not* as nice as a romantic hug." She went on to explain that it was sometimes hard to distinguish between a platonic and a romantic hug. The hugs with her friend Doug were not necessarily shorter or less intimate. Actually, *they involved about the same amount of body contact as a romantic hug.* She even talked during the hugs as she sometimes did with romantic hugs. "The only difference really is that our hands do not wander—they stay VERY still, in fact!"

This is an important point. Just as platonic kisses don't involve any tongue contact, platonic hugs usually don't involve any hand movement. In our culture, wandering hands signal more than friendly interest.

Does this mean that it's impossible to hug a friend of the opposite sex and have the hug remain platonic?

Not at all. Indeed, so many people enjoy friendly hugs with members of the opposite sex that this seems to be one of the most popular hugs. Survey reponses indicate that 98 percent of women and 94 percent of men occasionally hug friends of the opposite sex. These figures have to be qualified, however. Most people hug members of the opposite sex only in limited situations, such as when greeting a friend after a long separation. And they usually hug only very good friends of the opposite sex. As one twenty-four-year-old single woman from Maryland put it, "A hug isn't something I want to share with every Tom, Dick, and Harry. There has to be a connection with that male for me to want to hug him."

Would you like the opportunity to hug more members of the opposite sex without having to move on to other sex acts with them? If so, why don't you try this kind of hug more often?

WOMEN:

"I'd like more opportunities to hug my male friends, but I don't do it. I'm married, and my husband has repeatedly lectured me about giving guys the wrong impression, and I don't want to be perceived as a tease."

"Yes, I would. I don't try it more often because guys might misinterpret it. It's hard enough trying to show some people you're uninterested without giving them the wrong idea. Also, it can be uncomfortable hugging a guy who's just a friend when you're a woman and your chest gets in the way . . . maybe it's easier if you're flat-chested?"

"I'm sixteen and would love to have more opportunities to hug guy friends, but most of them aren't into hugging as much as girls and tend not to like it."

MEN:
"I want to hug everyone more. I have to emphasize that hugs are definitely not sexual for me or for most of my friends. There is a big difference between sex and intimacy. A hug means, 'I care about you and trust you.'"

"Yes, I'd like to. But some people are resistant. For example, a couple told me it's against their upbringing—they don't even hug their parents."

"The reason I don't hug more women friends—even though I'd like to—is that usually I don't feel I know them well enough to initiate a first hug. If they initiate hugs often enough, then I'll start initiating too."

How to keep hugs with friends of the opposite sex platonic

Some people try to keep these hugs purely platonic by preventing their hands from moving. After you get set into the hug—with your hands and arms gently holding the other person—stay still and don't move. As a twenty-five-year-old married woman from Illinois put it, "The hug remains platonic as long as the hands don't roam."

Another way is to limit body contact. According to a thirty-three-year-old woman, "Platonic hugs are shorter, less intimate, and involve less body contact." In other words, don't jam your pelvis into your partner. If you're a woman with big breasts, don't press them forcefully into the guy, especially if you're wearing a thin blouse and you know he'll feel everything.

A third way to make sure your hugs remain platonic is to keep them short. About 60 percent of people believe that friendly hugs are shorter than romantic ones. The longer you linger, the more your partner will think you've got romance on your mind. For example, friendly greeting hugs usually last only a few seconds.

Many people say things while giving a platonic hug. "Usually we are talking during the hug, saying things like 'see you soon!'" explains a thirty-three-year-old married woman. About 25 percent of men and women assume that talking during this hug will somehow keep it platonic. Maybe this is because they believe the other person will think, "He's talking, so he can't be too focused on me as a sexual object."

Probably the most cautious thing you can do is be certain *your* intent is purely platonic. That will help you keep things in perspective. According to Suzi Landolphi, author of *Hot, Sexy and Safer* (New York: Berkley, 1994), the most important thing in flirting is *not* to have any serious intent. Are you sure you don't want these hugs to lead to more intimate forms of contact? Would you be embarrassed if your lover saw you hugging your friend? If you think he or she would object, you may be getting too close to your special friend.

But then again, you have to use your own judgment. You can't let your lover be the *sole* determiner of your friendships, especially if he or she is overly possessive. For example, a twenty-five-year-old woman's husband discourages her from hugging *any* other men. This kind of total ban on harmless platonic contact is really too severe. After all, a little flirting now and then—some innocent platonic hugs—this is what life is all about!

What do women think about during platonic hugs?

You might be surprised if you could read a woman's mind during a platonic hug. Even though the actual physical contact may last only a few seconds, so many thoughts are careening through her mind that it would astound you. First of all, women usually worry that the man is going to misinterpret the hug as meaning something more than it does. Then they're doing fierce mental calculations to determine exactly how close you're pulling them toward your body. As a thirty-year-old married woman from California said, "I notice that male friends always try and get the breasts squished against their chest in this hug." She went on to say that this hug is just not easy to do. "There are so many things read into the hug that it becomes a bigger issue than need be. Often it is easier not to even try."

Sometimes women worry that they're getting more involved than they should. More often than not, they feel guilty about a hug like this. For example, when Nellie hugged Doug at the office she was thinking how nice it felt, but then afterward she said to herself, I shouldn't have done that because it felt *too* nice. And last but not least, women worry about what their boyfriends or lovers would think if they ever saw them hugging another man.

With all this emotional and intellectual turmoil, it's a little surprising that women hug platonic male friends at all.

What do men think about during platonic hugs?

Like most women, almost all men would like to have more friendly hugs. But at first, a man may not have enough courage to initiate one of these hugs, even with a good friend. He's often worried that he's getting too close too fast. He also worries that you may think he means more than he does with the hug. If and when he finally does work up the courage to hug you, he often worries that he's getting too physical with you and giving you the wrong impression about his intentions. For this reason, a guy who's a close friend may give you only a short little hug, one that doesn't seem friendly at all. But in the back of his mind he's often thinking, Wish I could hug her some more!

How do you initiate a platonic hug?

Sometimes they just happen, especially in greeting or saying good-bye. But more often than not, one party to the hug suggests it. A twenty-five-year-old woman had just spent a few hours together with a male friend. "When he went to leave, I asked if I could hug him," she explains. "He said yes, and we hugged. I always feel it's better to ask first rather than offend someone's sense of personal space."

If you're like most people, you probably would like more opportunities to hug your opposite-sex friends in a purely platonic way. But you worry that they'll misinterpret it. In truth, they probably feel the same way.

There will be times when a friend is in an emotional crisis and you can help with a platonic hug. There will come times when you need a way to say what words just can't say.

Say it with a platonic hug!

A young woman had a friend who was really depressed and writing suicide thoughts on his computer. "I gave him a hug," she says. "For me it was awkward, as I didn't really know what to do. For him it was great. He gave me a huge grin and said, 'Friends are really nice.' That was definitely a hug worth giving!"

The

$\mathcal{F}$AMILY HUG

"Stop it, Jack!" Brenda pushed her half-brother away. They were together in the house their mother rented every summer in Miami.

"Why?"

"I have to unpack and you're distracting me."

"You *love* being distracted."

"No, I *don't!*"

She broke free and went into the kitchen. Jack could hear her opening the refrigerator. He stood in the living room waiting. They were both in their midtwenties. This week they had the entire house to themselves.

For a full minute he stood perfectly still. He listened to her clinking glasses and silverware, but he wasn't going to follow her. He was thinking about the way she looked. She was wearing blue jeans and a white T-shirt.

When she came back into the living room she was carrying a glass of lemonade. She stopped abruptly. They stood facing each other for a long moment. She just looked at him, and then suddenly she smiled mischievously.

As if he had received a signal, Jack grabbed her around the waist. In one swift and easy motion he lifted her off her feet.

"Jaaaaaaaack!" she screamed in pleasure, holding the glass out to her side.

His arms were under her arms, his hands clasped behind her back. He spun her around and kissed her cheek. Then he put her down.

"I'm just happy to be on vacation with you."

"You don't have to break my ribs."

He sat on the couch and began to calm down. It was always exciting to see Brenda. Hugging her like that was a ritual with them. He did it whenever they saw each other after a long separation. It was his way of saying he loved her like a brother and also like *more* than a brother. But he never crossed the boundary and never really wanted to.

For her part, Brenda loved it when he paid attention to her like that. It made her feel special and loved. It also made her feel sexy in a flirtatious way. She knew they would never do anything more than hug playfully. But she often dreamed of finding someone who would hug her and play around and also respect her the way he did.

Jack and Brenda often share family hugs that are similar to the sensual hugs lovers exchange. At the other end of the spectrum are those dull little hugs you give relatives at large family gatherings. Filling the space between these two extremes is an array of family hugs ranging from the most affectionate to the most formal.

When you get right down to it, though, family hugs can really be divided into two varieties: hugs between parent and child, and hugs between everyone else. The parent-child hug is the foundation, the crucial basis of our sense of self-esteem. In recent clinical studies it was discovered that hugging and touch early in life are necessary for the development of a sense of self-worth and happiness.

For example, Harry F. Harlow's now classic studies of infant monkeys strongly suggest that those who are raised in isolation develop into neurotic animals. Monkeys raised with doll-like, cloth-and-wire mother surrogates were better adjusted than those raised in complete isolation. And those raised with their natural mothers were the best adjusted and most sociable of all. In 1959 Dr. Harlow wrote, "These results attest the importance—possibly the overwhelming importance—of bodily contact and the immediate comfort it supplies."

Other studies show that humans also need loving touch early in life to help them become social beings. According to Dr. Martha G. Welch, M.D., author of *Holding Time: How to Eliminate Conflict, Temper Tantrums, and Sibling Rivalry and Raise Happy, Loving, Successful Children* (New York: Simon & Schuster, 1988), children need to be hugged for extended periods of time. "In *holding time*, you physically embrace your child whether or not either of you feels, at that moment, the usual emotions that lead to an embrace. It does not necessarily begin with—but should never end without reaching—a happy phase of closeness. *Holding time* uses intense physical and emotional contact to reinforce the connection between you and your child." Dr. Welch goes on to encourage readers to hold their children until both parent and child are cuddling and snuggling and happy together.

Fostering the emotional bond between parent and child with hugs early in life will do much to ensure that children grow into more self-confident adults, says Dr. Welch.

Survey responses indicate that most adult children still hug their parents. "I hug my parents every time I see them, generally before they go to bed and whenever I need a hug and they are around," says a twenty-four-year-old woman from Maryland. This willingness to hug her parents was echoed by a twenty-five-year-old married woman from

Illinois: "I hug my parents all the time when I'm home (they live far away). I hug them in the kitchen, in the yard. It's just sort of 'Hello, I love you, I'm glad to be here.'"

Many men also enjoy a good hugging relationship with their parents. A Hawaiian student said, "I always hug my parents. They helped me cultivate the talent! The hugs are nurturing, protective, loving—bonding at its best."

But not everyone is so lucky. Some people find it difficult to hug one or both parents. Sometimes this difficulty starts early in life and leaves a crippling scar on the person's ability to give and receive affection from others.

"My mother and I don't get along real well," explains a woman in her thirties. "It's rough hugging her. It's very rough. Let me be honest here. She and I, we're not the best of friends, we're not real close. She tends to be very self-centered. It's hard to get close to her. There was a lot of rejection, including physical rejection, as a child growing up. That's just the way she is, and there's nothing I can do about it. And you get to the point where you don't want to get burned anymore. You try and try and it doesn't work, so you stop trying to hug after a while. I have a difficult time expressing my feelings for people even today."

Other individuals come from families that were not very physical. A nineteen-year-old Canadian woman never hugged her parents. A twenty-one-year-old woman blames her family's coldness for the lack of hugs in her early life. "My family's not a touchy-feely family, so I never hugged them much, and I hug them even less now that I'm an adult."

Luckily some people can get over a childhood of hug deprivation by hugging their parents on formal occasions, such as when greeting them or departing. "My family is not a close one, physical contact was limited," says a thirty-four-year-old woman from Ohio. "I hug my parents now because we don't see each other very often." Another young woman usually hugs her parents when she goes to visit them and again when she leaves. She finds these hugs "very comforting and reassuring." Most men also hug their parents when saying hello and good-bye. For example, a fellow from Canada said he rarely hugged his mother and father as a child, but now he hugs them "every time we meet."

Did you ever hug your parents? When? What was this hug like?

WOMEN:
"Yes, I have hugged my parents. I have a hard time hugging my father because I haven't felt very close to him. As for my mother, she's fairly affectionate and almost always is the first one to reach out for a hug at the end of a visit. I have no problems hugging her and like it very much because we are very close."

"I've always hugged my mother. My father I don't know very well. I didn't meet him until I was an adult. I hug my mom hello and good-bye and in between just because. With my father it's a more formal hug and doesn't happen every time we see each other. I can tell he isn't comfortable with it."

"I hug them when I'm cold or when we see each other after a long absence or before I leave to go back to my home 600 miles away."

"I hug both my parents—sometimes simultaneously! With my dad, I kind of had to teach him that it was okay to get close and make chest-to-chest contact, or to let the hug last more than just a few seconds. I think he was worried about long hugs seeming too sexual or something. Now he knows that *I* think it's okay, and so we're both more relaxed and natural about hugging."

"I love to hug my mom and was worried that she wouldn't want to do it any longer after she had a mastectomy. So I gave her no choice. I hugged her long and hard and close the first time I saw her after the operation, and now we're totally comfortable about it. I think it gives her a lot of self-confidence."

MEN:
"I hug them hello and good-bye. If I'm staying with them, I'll hug them before they go to bed (most of the time). It's always empowering to hug my parents."

"I hug them when I greet them and say good-bye. I hug them at birthdays and at Christmas. And sometimes I hug my mother for no particular reason other than to show her my love and affection. I like hugging both my parents."

"Not until lately. I think my parents' age was a factor. My dad was the one in the family to start asking for hugs. At first it felt awkward, but then that awkwardness disappeared and we hug more freely now."

"Yes, every time I see my mother after an extended absence, my father when I was much younger. It feels like a duty with my mother. My father endured it from me but didn't reciprocate."

"All the time; warm and affectionate. Occasionally indifferent (after arguments with my dad)."

Would you have liked more opportunities to hug your father?
WOMEN:
"Sometimes. I have a hard enough time as it is hugging him now. It's taken time for me to feel more and more comfortable with my father."

"My father died when I was about five years old, and before that my parents were separated. I would have liked more opportunities to hug him."

"By wanting more opportunities to hug my father I mean that I wish there were times when I could feel more loving toward him enough to *want* to hug him."

"I guess. But when you don't communicate well with your father, a hug isn't going to help. Communication must be there from the first, or the hug seems awkward."

MEN:
"Only when he's not with me and I see a touching, tender father-son movie or television show or see an actual father and son having a great time together."

"I would have liked for this kind of familiarity (hugging, other caresses) to have been a part of my family life from the start. As it is, we never got that kind of interaction until recent years."

"I would have liked more hugs as a child."

Would you have liked more opportunities to hug your mother?
WOMEN:
"Yes, I would. I don't think any amount of hugs would ever be enough."

"That isn't an issue because I do get to hug her every time I see her."

"No, we're on good communication terms, and we express our affection verbally."

MEN:

"No, because she gets a good mix of hugs from my sisters, father, and friends along with mine."

"Not really, unless she stops controlling."

"Sure!"

How to hug grandparents

Hugging your grandparents can actually give you some of their wisdom and life experience—there are people who swear it happens. Says a twenty-year-old male student, "I think that when you hug someone older, particularly a grandparent or relative, you get the sureness of a full life somehow expressed to you. It's very reassuring." Another man in his early thirties agrees: "I love hugging grandparents, people who are about twice as old, twice as smart and wise, and who have more of life under their belt. But I hug my parents more because they're around more. Plus I only have one remaining grandparent left."

Most people enjoyed hugging their grandparents so much you'd think they liked it more than hugging their parents. Many people *did* like it more and weren't afraid to admit it.

"I really enjoy hugging my grandparents," says a twenty-one-year-old woman from California. "There's just so much love there, and I don't see them very often, so hugs are infrequent."

Would you have liked more opportunities to hug your grandmother or grandfather?

WOMEN:

"My grandparents were wonderful people. But it's hard for me to be physically close to people that I'm emotionally close to. I know it makes no sense, but someone who I really love in my life—let's put it that way—it's hard for me to say 'I love you' and it's hard for me to express that, and so consequently with my grandparents I do hug them and everything, but it just takes a lot of effort and it's kind of hard for me to do it."

"I get to hug my maternal grandparents every time I see them. I have never (maybe once at my wedding) hugged my paternal grandmother and never met my paternal grandfather. So I would have liked the opportunity to hug both of them."

"Yes, but they live too far away for that to be possible."

MEN:
"No. Every time I saw them they usually gave me a hug (grandmothers more than grandfathers)."

"I loved hugging my grandmother. I used to hug her chubby body like a pillow and the great thing was that she always hugged me back with so much love—it was inexhaustible. Now that she's gone I sometimes miss her and wish I could still hug her."

How is hugging your grandparents different from hugging your parents?

WOMEN:
"It's different to the extent that I didn't see my grandparents day in and day out like my parents, so the hug is more of an I-haven't-seen-you-in-a-while hug."

"It was different because I knew they would spoil me and I'd get more attention, and also they smell and feel different. My grandfather is not the hugging type, but my grandmother is. She's real cuddly."

"My parents are obviously more affectionate with me."

"My mother's parents seem less controlling than she does, my father's parents seem perhaps obligated to do it."

"More formal, more for their sake than mine."

Hugging your children

We may not remember all those early hugs, but clinical psychologists claim that our childhood human contact leaves its mark on our nervous system and helps make us more confident and content adults. Children who are hugged are more likely to hug their own kids. One young man who received a lot of affection isn't a parent yet, but he says, "I've vowed that my kids will be hug-positive!"

Hugging children is so important that the HAVE YOU HUGGED YOUR CHILD TODAY? bumper sticker was a big seller in the 1980s and 1990s. But sometimes hugging a child can be a sad experience for the adult realizing that these hugs may be coming to an end. As the child grows into adulthood, hugging usually decreases. A thirty-four-year-old mother from Ohio says, "I hug my seven-year-old son often. Sometimes it makes me sad to hold him and realize how big he is and that soon he'll be too big for me to do this."

Hugging stepparents, stepkids, or half-brothers or -sisters

Not all relationships between stepparents or half-siblings are as smooth as that of Jack and Brenda. A young man who loves to hug remembers how odd it felt to hug his stepmother when he initially met her. "It was kind of eerie at first. Interesting in the sense that as I kept hugging my stepmother—long after she took on the half-title of being a mother—I could feel her slowly beginning to *really* take on the loving nature of a family member." A forty-year-old man remembers that his stepfather's hugs seemed "a little more distant at first."

A thirty-year-old medical student recalls her relationship with her half-brother. She did hug him a very long time ago, but not very often. "He isn't a touchy-feely person and hasn't ever seemed to be comfortable with contact." A young man explains how odd it was hugging his half-brother. "He thought I was weird at first, but thanks to my efforts and my father's, he's hug-active now."

The situation can be just as awkward for the stepparent hugging a stepchild. A thirty-five-year-old woman says, "I have two teenage stepdaughters who I've known since they were little. I would like to hug them more often, but sometimes I still feel like an outsider who has no place making that kind of contact with them."

How to initiate hugs with members of a blended family

One of the reasons for the popularity of *The Brady Bunch* television show is that it depicted a very successful blended family. The mother brought three girls into the family, the father three boys. In general, they interacted like a loving family more quickly than most blended families do in real life. Adapting to a new stepparent, -child, or -sibling isn't always such an instantaneous process. Here are suggestions for how to initiate hugs with members of your blended family.'

☛ Get to know the other person as an individual. Find out their likes and dislikes. This will give you an emotional understanding that will prepare you to hug them.

- Concentrate *only* on the individual you are hugging. Don't let yourself get distracted by comparisons to anyone else. For example, focus only on your stepmother when hugging her. Don't compare her in your mind to your biological mother.

- You may find it easier to initiate hugs in formal contexts at first. For example, when the person is going away on a vacation, or at their birthday party, or on New Year's Eve.

- Hug when greeting because this is expected. For example, give a stepparent who has just come home from work a greeting hug. Hug stepchildren when you return home from work.

- Tell your stepchildren that you want to start a daily family tradition of hugging them when they go off to school or tell them that *you* need a hug each morning before heading off to work.

- Always use memorable occasions—such as graduations, birthdays, making the honor roll, or landing a part in the spring play—as a time to hug.

- Hug stepparents goodnight. This is a painless way to break the ice.

- If a hug isn't expected, signal your intent by opening your arms out and approaching while saying something appropriate, such as, "Good night" or "You did such a great job on that school project!"

- In group situations, signal the fact that a hug is imminent by first hugging your blood relatives. On a holiday, for example, hug your brother and sister first. This will put stepsiblings on notice that this is accepted practice in your family. Next hug your stepsiblings the same way you hugged your other siblings.

The

UNREQUITED HUG

"Did you ever love anyone more than they loved you?"
Sharon was behind the wheel, driving to Florida for spring
break with her friend Eddie.

"Well, I guess so," he admitted.

"Tell me about it."

"I never told this story before because it was too embarrassing, but about five years ago I fell in love with a les-
bian."

Sharon turned to look at him.

"And you still fell in love with her?"

"Yes. There was something about her that attracted me.
She was so nice, so kind, so beautiful that I couldn't help
falling in love with her."

"Even though you knew it could never go anywhere?"

"Yes."

"So what happened?"

"Well, one summer I went to visit her. She lived in
Florida in a house with another girl—her lover. It was horrible visiting them but I was so infatuated I put up with it."

"It must have been traumatic for you."

"Of course it was traumatic, especially when she told me
she was moving to London. I was devastated. I was in emo-

tional shock for two months, anticipating the day she would be leaving the country forever."

"What did you do?"

"On the day she was scheduled to leave, I went to her house to help her pack. Then she came outside with her luggage to wait for the cab, and she said good-bye. I told her I wanted to hug her. I was still in love with her. And I was hoping to dissuade her from leaving by showing her how much I cared for her. What a fool I was."

"What happened?"

"I gave her a long slow hug there on the sidewalk in front of her building. As I held her, she started to cry. I think she liked me a lot more than she ever admitted. I tried to get her to stay by hugging her and telling her I loved her. It was a horrible time. She told me not to make a scene. But when she finally got into the cab, I started screaming, 'Don't go!' and I actually ran into the street after the cab yelling, 'Don't leave me!'"

By this point Sharon was laughing in spite of herself.

"I'm sorry, Eddie. You're serious?"

"Yes, I was crazy about her. And hugging her made me think I was going to get a chance to make her see how much I loved her. But she didn't respond. I did the best I could, but she left me. That was the most painful hug I ever experienced."

Like Eddie, most people have hugged someone who broke their heart. This unrequited hug can be one of the most awkward romantic experiences of your young life—or of your *old* life if, like the great German poet Goethe, you fall in love with someone who's eighteen when you're fifty-eight. Hugs like this can ruin a hugging career if you let them. But why should you? Everyone who has lived a full life has encountered these gut-wrenching embraces at one time or another. So don't let a few unrequited hugs get the better of you. Just look at all the other people who have suffered through the same agony and try to take comfort in the fact that the heart is meant to be broken a few times during a typical love life.

Have you ever hugged someone you loved more than they loved you (an unrequited hug)? What was this like?

WOMEN:
"Yes. It was *not* a nice feeling! I didn't feel hugged back, and this made me feel rejected."

"Uncomfortable is the best word to describe it."

"Yes, and it's difficult. You are obviously holding onto someone who doesn't want you, and you can feel it."

MEN:
"Yes, and it was obvious they had no enthusiasm."

"Very shallow. Very unfulfilling."

"This hug had an empty feeling to it."

How to survive an unrequited hug

You gnash your teeth and your palms sweat. You realize you're hugging someone who doesn't love you back. They feel like a sandbag they're so insensitive. Or maybe they feel sensual and supremely sexy—yet they don't seem to be responding to your longing embrace. What do you do? How do you get through the experience?

According to most people who answered the hugging survey, you just have to grin and bear it. There's no use trying to change things when you're engaged in an unrequited hug. But this isn't the answer you'd get from Ovid. In *The Art of Love* the Roman poet encouraged young lovers to pursue the man or woman of their dreams and never give up. His book is filled with advice for capturing the hearts of those who are cold, who spurn your love, who give you unrequited hugs.

And this isn't the advice you'll get from me, either. I'm not going to tell you to grin and bear it. I'm telling you to go out there and give that unrequited hug all you've got. Hug them back like your life depended on it. Give them a hug they'll never forget. Put them to shame with your hugging technique!

Now, here's one secret most people never realize: That person giving you the unrequited hug—that person who supposedly *doesn't* love you—*is* involved with you on some physical level. Otherwise they wouldn't even be hugging you! And if that's the case, you might as well try and enjoy the hug as best you can. In other words, wrap your arms tight around them and get all you can from the physical contact while it lasts. Don't feel sorry for yourself! Make *them* feel sorry they ever said good-bye to *you*.

As one twenty-four-year-old woman said, an unrequited hug is "a feeling of enjoyable pain." So why not enjoy the enjoyable part of it while you can?

Don't avoid unrequited hugs!

Some people are so squeamish about emotional hurt they shy away from all life's great experiences. They see an unrequited hug coming, they close their eyes and run in the opposite direction. For instance, a woman in her early twenties never gets into a position where she'll be involved in an unrequited hug. "If I know the other person doesn't like me as much as I like them, I avoid situations where my extra emotions will show. And hugging's one of those situations." In other words, she tries to avoid hurt by avoiding contact.

This is a big mistake.

Better to jump right in and take unrequited hugs whenever you can. Why deny yourself the pleasure of a warm physical embrace with someone of the opposite sex who you consider ultimately huggable?

Here's another secret most people don't realize. An unrequited hug today may turn into a requited hug tomorrow. This means that if you hug someone who doesn't love you today—and if you can give them a nice, good, warm, technically competent hug—they're very likely to rethink their feelings toward you and start to want to hug you in the future!

For example, a young man said that after *one* lonely unrequited hug with a woman he loved, he eventually started enjoying some *normal* hugs with her. "I had an unrequited hug with a close woman friend who I'd been pursuing a romantic relationship with off and on for several years. I finally told her that I loved her. She said she wanted nothing more than a friendship. We hugged. I felt sad and lonely because she didn't love me. We hugged a lot before that hug and after, too. That hug was the *only* sad lonely one." This is progress! Who knows where this will lead?

So don't avoid unrequited hugs. You can never tell when they might open the door to new romance.

The

ℬEAR HUG

All you feel is the heat like a dull slap in the face that knocks you off balance until you just want to go somewhere air-conditioned. You knew it would be hot near the equator, but you honestly didn't expect—

"One hundred and four degrees, señor."

When you finally get to the hotel you breathe a sigh of relief. You're not even *thinking* of touching another human being until you cool down.

Here you are in a hotel in Ponta de Pedras at the mouth of the mighty *Amazonas* facing piranhas and sunstroke outside. And Charleen inside.

Charleen is taking a shower. You're pressing yourself against the cold-air duct waiting for her. When she comes out, she's dressed in white shorts and a blouse. You wonder what she's thinking.

You've been leaning up against the cooling unit so long your sweat has evaporated and your back feels like ice. Charleen is putting on lipstick. You go up to her. She looks like she's cooled down some. You're slowly getting back to normal yourself. So when she turns from the mirror you smile slyly, as if to say, "It's just the two of us here in the wilds of Brazil, honey. So let's forget the fight we had last week and enjoy ourselves, okay?"

But what does she do?

Slowly she steps up to you and puts her slender arms around your waist. And gives you a hug so tight you can't inhale! A vicious embrace that makes you think any minute you're going to hear your vertebrae snap.

You wonder where she ever got the strength to hug like this. But the hug itself isn't what's really worrying you. It's her attitude that confuses you. What does it mean? Why is she hugging you so hard? Why is she trying to crack your ribs?

That's the beauty of this hug, though. A bear hug can always mean either of two diametrically opposite things. It can mean I love you so goshdarn much I wanna squeeze you into me and make us one. Or it can mean I want to break your back you good-for-nothing lout, you get on my nerves and deserve to be pulverized!

Keep that in mind the next time you get, or give, a bear hug.

As one twenty-six-year-old from Coventry, England, put it, "When you hug your girl in anger or jealousy you don't give a normal hug. It's more of a bear grip."

But then there's the flip side.

As a thirty-three-year-old married woman explains, "Really tight hugs are loving and playful." And as another young woman said, "If a hug has a lot of pull in it, it means you're trying to get really close to your partner."

So Davie could intrepret this either way. Charleen may be expressing her hidden anger by squeezing all the air from his lungs. Or she may be saying, "We're far from home. Let's get closer than ever!"

Because of its dual nature, a bear hug is uniquely suited to allowing you to tell your partner how you feel about how they feel. For example, if Charleen is still angry, and Davie is right in interpreting her bear hug as a sign of anger, then he can do any of a number of things in response. He can let her know that he's angry too, by squeezing her like he means to crush her. Or he can give her a loving bear hug in return.

Never forget that while the bear hug can be a contentious hug, it can also express great love. People give bear hugs to relatives or friends who've just been rescued from danger. When a prisoner of war is finally released, family members give the liberated person bear hugs. It's a sure way to say, "We love you so much we don't ever want to let go again."

A young man recently engaged confirmed this loving quality of the bear hug. "We give each other bear hugs when we're very happy, like after a particularly romantic moment." His bear hugs typically continue "until one of us turns blue and starts pounding."

A bear hug is also a test of trust. You have to trust your partner not to hurt you. As another young man put it, "I guess at times it could be physically painful, but in an odd way that might be part of the attraction. We trust each other to squeeze that hard, knowing that it's not meant to be harmful."

There are plenty of nuances to the bear hug. When trying it, notice carefully how your partner reacts. A particular bear hug can be breathtaking and hurtful. Or playful and *very* loving.

And sometimes you'll swear it's a little of both.

The
$\mathcal{P}$UBLIC HUG

Eric is a transfer student from Oslo and the most gorgeous-looking guy in school. Blond hair, blue eyes, a face like a god. Megan just loves being with him, despite the fact that her parents don't approve. They're always reminding her that he's going back to Norway at the end of the school year and she'll never see him again.

At seven-thirty she leaves the house and drives to the Campus Bowling Alley. Everything about the night is supremely romantic. She runs up to him, and immediately they're in each other's arms.

They never do talk much when they're out on a date—they mostly just hug and kiss. And a lot of their hugging is done in public.

He's got his arm around her and is nestling his cheek against the side of her face. Megan's eyes flick up to the windows. It's so risky! If her father saw them together she'd be in big trouble. Luckily the only people here tonight are some college kids and a few younger students.

There's a room in back with tables and video games and after a while they go in there and sit at a booth. Eric puts his arm around her. Megan acts like nothing is happening. Later they get two ice cream sodas. She sips hers through a straw and lets Eric hug her until she wants to leave with him to go somewhere more exciting.

Outside on the sidewalk he kisses her. Some kids pass by and look. Across the street a group of college girls gawk in envy. What a thrill it is to be with him!

Then they're in the car again. She leans her head on his shoulder. Parked right in front of the bowling alley, she lets him kiss her and hug her. Every once in a while kids walk by and stare at them. It's fun to be seen like this! Maybe she does have a wild side to her like her parents are always saying. Maybe she has a streak of exhibitionism in her.

"Let's go on the roof, Eric. It'll be great. Come on!"

She gets out and leads him by the hand around the back of the building up the fire escape onto the roof.

Now it's even more romantic! For a while she's worried about people passing by. Anyone down on the other side of the street can look up and see them. But really it's the mere *possibility* of danger that excites her. Impulsively she opens her coat and steps up to him.

She's wearing a short skirt. The wind whips through her legs. She puts her arms around his waist. He grabs onto her like he's afraid she might fall off the roof. Her heart begins to race. She might be discovered at any minute! These public hugs are getting her excited. She wants Eric to do *more* than hug her. She presses her hips into him and pulls him close.

"Hold me tighter, Eric!"

"Huh?"

"Don't talk! Just *hold* me."

"What if people look up and see?"

"So what?"

She's sure he'll do whatever she says. And she wants to do something crazy with him now, something totally different and extraordinary. Something she'll remember long after he's gone.

Megan isn't alone in thinking that public hugs are the ultimate in hugging fun. Close to 100 percent of people in our sample reported that they like to hug in public, many of them raving about the experience. Why? What is it about hugging on the roof of a bowling alley at nine o'clock at night that sends shivers down a young girl's spine?

"I like people to know that I have someone to hug!" explains a seventeen-year-old girl from Massachusetts. "I feel . . . well, not *proud* exactly, but . . . like saying, 'Hey, look at me!'" Other people echoed this desire to show off for the world. "I love hugging in public," says a woman from California. "I feel very close to my partner when it happens, probably because I'm not embarrassed at other people seeing this."

Then there are those who like public hugging because it allows them to create a pocket of romantic isolation in the midst of a crowd. "I love hugging in public and feel like my boyfriend and I are the only two people in the world," writes a twenty-four-year-old woman. When hugging in public, many people become oblivious to the environment, lost in their own special universe. "When you're that close to someone, you forget the people around you," says one young woman. "For that brief moment in time, everybody else just drops out and becomes invisible. Also it makes me feel secure because I *know* someone and I'm not totally alone, even if it is only an acquaintance."

People who admit that they like public hugs aren't the self-conscious type. They're usually extroverted and self-confident. "I'm not self-conscious," says a young man who enjoys hugging in public. "Perhaps I like to feel proud that I have so many close friends and a lover that I can hug."

This is the key to enjoying public hugs. You have to feel happy about showing off. Probably you've got to have a trace of the exhibitionist in you. And you've got to want to create a little haven of romance with your partner despite the occasional onlooker who may pass by and rubberneck.

Where to hug in public

Not everyone is bold enough to climb up to the roof of a bowling alley and hug away in plain view of the city. But you don't have to go to these extremes. I asked people where they liked to hug in public and their answers were remarkably pedestrian. They enjoy public hugs in semi-public places such as supermarkets (in the less-crowded aisles), backs of churches, subway platforms, clubs, beaches, stores, restaurants, streets, bars, parks, telephone booths—*telephone booths*? Well, you name it. "Oh, please, after all that, I don't think you really want a detailed list!" writes a man in his early twenties who loves hugs.

Many people didn't even bother cataloguing all the spots where they had enjoyed public hugs. It would go on too long. "Everywhere!" or "Just about everywhere!" were common replies to this question.

How to hug in public when your partner doesn't like to

Keep in mind that your partner may be a bit more reticent than you. "I like hugging in public, but my partner doesn't," says a young woman from New Zealand. "I guess I feel awkward when we hug in public because I know he doesn't enjoy it, although I do."

The best suggestion is to take it easy at first. Try hugging in places that are public but deserted. For example, a vacant parking garage or a street corner when no one is on the street but the two of you. Once you've mastered these easy semipublic hugs, you'll be ready for some advanced exercises.

Your next step is to try hugging in public when people are visible further off in the distance. Try hugging on a street when people are at the other end of the block. Or you could hug in a car where you're protected from onlookers by lots of steel and glass.

Your final step is to hug in a crowded area when other people are very close. If you can do this with calm nerves and actually enjoy the experience, you're hugging with the best of them.

Advanced public hugging

Once you've mastered the basic public hug, you'll really start to have fun. If you thought your hugging days were over, if your hugs don't have the same excitement now that they once had, just start to see the world in a slightly different light. Raise your consciousness by looking at every new place you visit as a potential hugging location.

For instance, in a bank you can often stand incredibly close to your partner while on line, and if you act nonchalant no one will notice a thing. Sneak up behind her and just rest your chin on her shoulder, putting one hand gingerly and slowly around her waist. Gently, so gently she hardly notices you're there! Play games like this to see how close you can get without giving yourselves away.

Keep in mind that you don't want to antagonize people. But don't worry too much about them either. Usually you won't annoy anyone. Nearly 100 percent of people who answered the survey said they don't mind if other people hug in public. "I *wish* other people *would* hug in public!" said a fellow in his midtwenties who loves hugging.

If you want to know the truth, however, most people *say*

they don't mind if others hug in pubic, but many of them will start to feel jealous when they see how much you're enjoying it. "If I have a relationship, I think public hugging is wonderful," says one young woman. "If I'm single I hate it because I'm jealous." And a young man writes, "I used to feel sad and lonely when I didn't have a girlfriend and saw a couple hugging in public." A sixteen-year-old girl echoes these sentiments. "I think it's cute, but often I feel jealous."

Sometimes you can have more fun in public by *not* going too far but instead hugging subtly and cautiously when others don't even know you're doing it. "Keep it tasteful and cuddly, not graphic," recommends a young married woman from Sacramento.

How do public hugs differ from private hugs?

WOMEN:

"Private hugs feel much more intimate. It's weird to see tight public hugs because you don't know whether or not you should stare at them (since you *want to* see) or pretend you don't see them."

"Mine tend not to be different, except for maybe shorter and without wandering hands."

MEN:

"No one notices but yourself and her when you're in private. You can hug any part of your partner's body in any position. Public hugs are more conservative. Sometimes my hands will start to wander and she'll let me know whether it is all right or not before they do start to wander. I glance around to see if any people are looking."

"I think private hugs are closer to intimate sharing, while public hugs are partially a declaration of affection."

ℋOLDING HANDS

The Beatles sent shock waves through the music world on February 16, 1964 when they appeared live on *The Ed Sullivan Show* and sang their first U.S. Top 40 hit, "I Want to Hold Your Hand" before an audience of 73 million people. The 2½-minute song described the simple act of holding hands in phrases so dripping with sensuality that fans responded immediately, buying an unprecedented 1.5 million copies in the first five days after its release. As everything about the song implies, there's a lot more to holding hands than simply holding hands.

More than 90 percent of survey respondents said they enjoy holding hands. Most had stumbled upon the joys of hand-holding by chance, since there's very little written about the subject. Indeed, this chapter contains the first compilation of pointers on every aspect of hand-holding for modern lovers.

When to hold hands

Have you ever wondered whether you should hold hands with someone? A good way to answer that question is to keep in mind that *the best time to hold hands is in a crowded area.* The reason is simple. Crowds serve as the perfect excuse for holding hands. Of course you can hold hands when no one else is around, but that's a purely private act. Hold hands on a crowded street and you'll get a private *and* a public thrill. "Sometimes we hold hands when we're alone together, but usually it's more for public display," explains a young woman from Omaha. There's a little exhibitionist in everyone." Go ahead and hold hands in public, that's half the fun.

Where to hold hands

- In a theater when you're sitting together
- When boarding a subway train
- When crossing a busy street
- On a crowded sidewalk
- In a department store
- On a dance floor

How to make initial contact

The area most fraught with difficulty for neophytes is how to make that initial contact. You may be nervous, but a little nervousness can even add to your enjoyment. Remind yourself that it is appropriate to hold hands on the first date. Then make that initial contact like this:

- Wait until you're in a crowd. "We usually hold hands when walking through crowds," says a woman in her twenties. "That way we don't lose each other."

- ☞ Get close. For example, if you're both walking on a busy sidewalk, walk so close that your shoulders and arms touch. Your hands may also brush together.
- ☞ Keep walking but glance down to see where your partner's hand is.
- ☞ Spread your fingers wide so you don't miss when you make your move.
- ☞ Make contact by gently grasping your partner's hand.

What happens if your date pulls away or gets insulted? Don't become alarmed. You've simply made your move too soon. About 20 percent of people surveyed said that their partner rejected hand-holding. One twenty-year-old woman from Connecticut said, "I have never had someone react negatively. I, however, have pulled away when someone who was too aggressive tried to hold my hand." Other women will allow a man to hold their hand even if they don't like it, so as not to make a scene. A young woman from Massachusetts said, "If I didn't want to hold a guy's hand I would still do it, so as not to cause attention or embarrassment."

Did you ever try to hold hands with someone and have them react negatively by slapping you, pulling away, or telling you to stop? Or did you ever react that way?

WOMEN:

"I can only remember one time when someone pulled away when I wanted to hold hands. I, on the other hand, pull away a lot."

"I usually ask to stop, and hold his belt loop instead."

"Only when fighting."

"Yes. My husband never liked to hold hands, and he told me candidly that he didn't like it."

Do you ever ask before holding hands?

Only about 15 percent of people ask before holding hands.

WOMEN:

"No, the moment of anticipation is a lot better. I never know what to say or do."

"No, because the men I date will usually ask me."

"No, but on our first few dates my boyfriend did, which I found awkward."

"I usually ask in a general way, for example, 'Do you like holding hands?'"

What technique do you like for hand-holding?

MEN:

"We mostly just hold lightly, occasionally squeezing. As we walk, we usually—and I think artfully—change configurations (to keep down sweat and to caress each others' hands). I'd say we more often hold palms than mixing fingers."

"A loose fit with fingers intertwined if the weather is hot."

WOMEN:

"You really have to develop a style with each partner. With some of my ex-boyfriends, intertwined fingers hurt, so we didn't hold hands that way. With my husband, that's perfectly comfortable, but sometimes we don't intertwine. The grip tends to be not too loose and not too tight."

"I prefer a loose fit with fingers *not* intertwined, with an occasional squeeze."

What do you like about holding hands?

WOMEN:

"It always makes me feel like he can read my mind when he holds my hand."

"I like the warmth of his hands and the innocence of hand-holding."

"It's a silent way to say, 'I love you.'"

MEN:

"I like to squeeze hard, to transmit a sense of power and stability to my mate."

"I love holding hands, but not as much as walking arm in arm."

Some people just can't stand being the center of attention. They feel like they're under a spotlight when they hold hands, especially if they're around people they know. "I have problems holding hands in public," says a teenager from California. "I think partly because my college is all women, so when you hold hands with a guy you feel like everyone's staring at you or something. But at places where I don't know anyone I hold hands a lot more."

Is there anything you dislike about hand-holding?

WOMEN:

"Occasionally it's embarrassing."

"Not really! Unless you need to do something like—oh, I don't know—scratch your nose? Then it's kind of awkward to do that if you have something in your other hand and scratch using the hand that's in your partner's!"

"I dislike holding hands when our palms become sweaty."

"I prefer to walk with our arms around each other, it's more intimate."

MEN:
"I like to stop holding hands when our hands start to get really sweaty."

"I hate holding hands when our friends are around."

Please describe a time when you held hands.

WOMEN:
"The night before my boyfriend first left for college, he and I went on a date. We joked for a while about what he would do when he was away in New Hampshire (drink, party, meet girls, you name it.). The joking led to a fight, so I took his right hand and held it between my two hands as a reassurance that I knew he wouldn't do anything to jeopardize our relationship. He understood and smiled."

"I first met my boyfriend at a nightclub. We hit it off immediately and spent the evening talking and dancing. We got along so well that we didn't notice that our friends had left the club. We took a cab to the end of my street. He walked me to my door and it felt very natural when he reached for my hand. His holding my hand showed me that he liked me, that he respected me, and that he was a gentleman. Any other physical contact at that time would have been inappropriate. Holding hands was a safe, comfortable way of physically expressing that we liked each other."

"At the funeral of my boyfriend's grandmother, I found it very difficult to express how sorrowful it felt. It hurt to see him in such pain, and I didn't know how to show it. At one point, while sitting side by side during the service, he grabbed my hand and held it so tight I knew my presence was a comfort to him."

MEN:

"When I was twenty-seven I went to an art show with a good-looking woman who was a few years older. I thought it was strictly a business outing because we both worked together in the publicity department and we were scouting out some artwork. But as soon as we got there she started holding my hand. It was a funny feeling, very exciting and nerve-racking too because I was going out with someone else at the time and didn't want to be seen holding hands with this other woman."

Do's and don'ts of hand-holding

DO:

☞ Lead your partner hither and thither. He or she will follow willingly.

☞ Allow your partner to take the lead. Be a willing follower.

☞ Let your hands occasionally break apart. Then after a short while reestablish contact.

☞ Give your partner a squeeze now and then.

DON'T:

☞ Don't squeeze your partner's hand in a viselike grip. "I don't like really tight hand-holding where your fingers feel like they'll break," says one teenager.

☞ Don't tug violently.

☞ Don't worry if your hand gets sweaty. It happens to the most experienced lovers, especially on hot days.

Holding hands when alone together

Sure, the *best* place to hold hands is in public. But you can also hold hands when you're alone together. Why would you want to do this? Well, some people find it an intimate way to maintain contact when they're out of the public eye. "We hold hands when we're watching television and there's an emotional moment that affects both of us," says a teenager from California. And some people even prefer holding hands when they're alone. "I hold hands with my boyfriend much more often when we're alone," says another teen. "We just stand facing each other and hold both hands while talking."

In fact, there are more people holding hands in private than you might realize. Some of them even put up with significant logistical problems to do so. "I'm shorter than my boyfriend," writes one young woman. "So when we hold hands standing alone at home or when strolling along together, it feels awkward. It's especially hard for us to hold hands while walking."

When you can put up with problems like that, you know you've really got something worth holding onto.

The

LEG HUG

You say your boyfriend likes to hug your legs. *It's so weird!* When you lie down he lies next to you with his head near your stomach and his arms around your thighs. You could be wearing jeans or slacks or even painter pants and he still loves it. And if you're in a short skirt he loses his mind entirely when he hugs your legs. It's enough to make you think he's obsessed. How do you explain something like that?

But when you stop to think about it you have to admit that you like it when he rests his hand on your thigh or knee. Thighs are a great part of the body to hug. You have to admit *that* at least. So why do you get so nervous sometimes when he hugs your legs?

"It's a sensual hug," says a young woman from Virginia. "It can be romantic if done gently. But when you start getting up near my thighs I can take the hug either of two ways: as romantic and tender, or as getting into the realm of the sexual. So I often don't know how to react. Sometimes I get turned on by it and sometimes I don't."

Romantic leg hugs

The only reason legs aren't hugged more often in a romantic context is that the arms—the chief means of hugging—can't reach them when you're standing. When you sit or lie down, however, all that changes. Your legs are then within reach and become fair game for romantic hugs. "I like it when he's sitting on a chair and I'm sitting on the floor next to him," says a married woman in her early thirties. "I hug his thigh and lean against his lower legs."

"When we're in a restaurant," says a young woman in law school, "my boyfriend sometimes rests his hand on my thigh. No one notices. Its not sexual. It's intimate, secret, and romantic. And it makes me feel closer to him—it calms me down. In fact, when we're out together and he hugs me like that I never need a drink."

Sitting next to each other while watching television is another time when many people get tangled up in romantic leg hugs. "Often her back is up against the couch and it's hard to snake my hand behind it to hug her around the waist, so I like to hug her thigh," says one young man. "I like to hug my husband's knee or thigh in the car or when we're sitting next to each other on a couch," says a woman from Memphis.

Keep in mind that when a man hugs your legs he's often returning to a feeling of childhood bliss. Take a look at any toddler. Notice the way the kid hugs his mother's calves, pressing his face into her. Studies show that children become more secure after contact with their mother's body and after experiencing the comforting and familiar smell of mother. So, let your lover regress a little!

"Sometimes I wriggle lower in bed to waist-height and cuddle with one of her legs like a child would his mother's, just because it feels nice," says a young man from the Southwest. "Other times, when we're at a restaurant, she crosses her leg over mine so I can half-hug it toward me. In my opinion, I don't get my legs hugged nearly as often as I'd like!"

"Why is he always pressing his nose into my feet?" says one young woman. Probably because the scent of socks and stockings adds to his pleasure during a leg hug. Some women are outraged by this possibility. But one reluctant young woman said, "I put my own stockings to my nose one day to see what my husband was raving about, and what do you know? It smelled like perfume! No wonder he loves hugging my legs and feet."

One young man even suggested a return to the *womb* during a contortionist hugging experience. "We were in bed after making love. I was on my side, my head on her upper thigh, my shoulder between her legs, my arms wrapped around her thigh. Her leg was between my two legs. I was in somewhat of a fetal position." Ah, the pleasures of returning to the source!

You say your boyfriend is encouraging you to try the latest fashion in women's stockings? You've seen it on MTV and in magazines. It's called the *thight*, a thigh-high stocking that stays up by itself. You wear it with a miniskirt and there's a patch of bare flesh showing between the top of the *thight* and the hem of your skirt. So you tried it once and all he wanted to do was hug your legs?

You never made it to the nightclub?

The guy is definitely out-of-his-mind crazy about these leg hugs. What is it with guys, anyway?

The

$\mathcal{S}$ EXUAL HUG

"Any time is a good time for a hug, even in the throes of passion," says a young man in his twenties. "It's an excellent way to catch your breath, at the very least. It's very sensual; a great pause to kiss and exchange vows."

When I asked "What advice can you offer to the opposite sex about hugging before, during or after sex?" one medical student in her midtwenties said, "Do it! Especially *after*, as that often gets neglected. Hugging after sex adds a lot of emotion to the physical act."

I included other questions in the survey, such as "Do you like hugging your lover when they are partly undressed?" "What clothes or underclothes do you like him or her to be wearing during a hug?"

I was surprised to find that women liked this as much as men. "Yes, just his briefs," said a happily married woman in her thirties. "I love it when we hug and he's in his silk boxer shorts," said a teacher in her twenties.

Other women preferred hugging totally naked. Said one, "Hugging my bare-chested lover, when I too am bare-chested, is my favorite. The touching of our hot skin together feels incredible."

Not surprisingly, guys loved hugging women who were

partly undressed. "I love hugging her when she's wearing just underwear," says a guy in his early twenties. "Sometimes it's the most erotic hug of all, yet the sweetest." And a thirty-year-old man from Washington, D.C., writes, "I like hugging her when she's in her panties and her sweatshirt, other times just her SOCKS!"

I also asked whether people liked to hug with *massage oil* on their bodies. (These oils are available in most health food stores or sex stores. Usually they are plain soybean oil or almond oil, and they're often scented with musk, sandalwood, or other fragrances.) The answers to this one surprised me—so few people seem to know about the fun of oil massages. Only 10 percent of women and 25 percent of men said they hugged when using massage oil. One fellow who knew about it said, "Hugging with oil on your body is like wearing satin. Even though it's scarcely on you, it still feels like it's going to slip off. Likewise being covered with oil; even though you have a firm hug around your partner, you feel like you're going to slip right off each other."

More people are aware of the slippery effect of hugging with *soap* all over their naked bodies. This is a common practice when couples shower together. "We never used oil, but we have used soap during hugging," says one young woman. "Sure, we hug with oil on our bodies," says a young man who loves hugging. "It's a bit messier, but just as fun as with a soapy body."

Finally I asked what other hugging practices people enjoyed when they got sexual with their partners. Here are their responses broken down by sex.

What turns guys on when hugging?

Men like hugging a fully clothed woman who presses her chest to theirs. "I like to feel her breasts against me, even if she's wearing a shirt or sweater," says a guy in his twenties. And despite all the talk about the no-bra look, 82 percent of guys also like to feel a girl's bra under her shirt when they hug her.

What turns women on when hugging?

Guys, keep in mind that virtually any part of a woman's body can give her erotic pleasure during a hug. One especially sensitive area is the chest, even if she's wearing a bra and blouse. Almost 85 percent of women get turned on when you hug them fully clothed and press your chest to theirs. Says a student, "The feel of his chest against mine—even when I'm fully dressed—is sensual and intimate and highlights our differences physically."

One quarter of the women sampled even enjoy the feeling of their own bra against their breasts while hugging. So the best technique to follow is to press your chest into her breasts so that you can feel her bra against the front of your chest. This ensures that you are putting enough pressure into the hug to stimulate her.

One twenty-four-year-old woman who didn't like this explained why. "I hate the feeling of my bra, period, and try not to wear one when I can get away without it, such as by wearing a bulky sweater, a sweatshirt, or lots of layers."

About 75 percent of women get turned on when hugging in just their underwear. These women say that they get a thrill from hugging in their bra and panties, often because there's plenty of skin contact as well as an element of mystery. Says one young woman, "It's fun because you have bare skin contact, but there's still that hidden, most intimate part of you." And another woman echoed a feeling expressed by many, "It's a sort of freedom feeling, enough to get my boyfriend and me aroused momentarily, and it can lead to more if we want it to."

Although only 27 percent of women spank their partners while hugging, 66 percent get turned on when their boyfriends spank them playfully. One young woman in her early thirties says, "He often spanks me while hugging, and it's meant to be a playful act. Never hard enough to really hurt. And he does it while standing or sitting, but usually standing." Another woman in her early twenties says, "He sometimes spanks me during sex and I don't mind this. I actually enjoy it because I know it's playful. He generally doesn't spank me otherwise. However, he very frequently pats my behind and I love this. It is a game between the two of us. Or sometimes instead of a pat he will just rest his hands on my bottom while hugging. This is a ritual we both enjoy and it makes us feel loved."

Advice for men

Many women consider hugs romantic, not sexual. So take the time to hug her in a romantic way more often, without trying to push ahead into the realm of sex. You'll find that she appreciates this a great deal and is more affectionate toward you. You may also find that she is more eager to have *sex* if you start out with a purely *romantic* approach.

The
$\mathscr{M}$OVING HUG

You're at your first high school dance with a date. He's a nice boy, but you can't believe he knows any real dance steps. He leads you in front of the band a little awkwardly. At first you're bored and you just stand there leaning against him, shuffling your feet this way and that. It feels nice to have his arms around you, though. It's such an unusual sensation to feel a warm body against yours. For some reason you've got butterflies in your stomach. You begin paying attention to the music, a romantic song you like. And then without warning it happens. It starts feeling good to be with him. Frighteningly good. In fact, you can't remember if you've ever experienced anything like this before. You hold him tighter, as if your body was created for the express purpose of hugging him. What a funny feeling! By the time the song is over your heart is pounding and your palms are sweaty with nervous energy.

During a moving hug something exciting usually happens. The contact of your partner's body changes ever so subtly and deliciously. You can feel it in your legs like an invitation to tango. If you're slow-dancing really close you can feel it like a fire in your hips. Hugging on the go always adds a jolt of provocation to any normal hug.

Dancing hugs

Most people thoroughly enjoy hugging when slow dancing. "I go dancing a lot," says a young man from New York. "And as the evening moves on we touch and hug more. It's very arousing because we're moving to the music and our bodies are touching. I think a nightclub is one place in public where you can be really wild. A lot of couples are hugging while dancing also."

"It's like a simple, informal slow dance," writes a young computer analyst, "we don't worry about steps—just being close and swaying to the music."

This is probably one of the easiest hugs to do. Simply hold onto your partner and take tiny steps, first one way, then the other. "Dancing, slow dancing, is really one long moving hug, which is why I love it so much," writes a teenager.

The umbrella hug

This one is especially popular in tropical climates. "Brother, you don't know what you're asking," writes a young man from Hawaii. "Hilo is the wettest city in the country. It rains about three hundred days of the year . . . do we know umbrellas! For an umbrella hug, we just walk arm in arm a *little* closer than usual. Often it's my left torso behind her back, tilting my head against hers."

The umbrella hug is also practiced in the Northeast, as one young man from Hartford reports. "A few times in the past year we've hugged under one. I'll hold the umbrella in my left hand with my arm around her waist and her arm around mine. It's another excuse to get close. During some downpours I'd like to hug without an umbrella—probably a tight bear hug!"

The moving hug

Sometimes you move during a hug with no real reason except that it feels good. Of course, either partner can initiate it.

"Occasionally when we hug, my wife pushes me back against the bed and flops down on top of me," writes a young man from Mexico. "She has other things on her mind and our hug is the prelude to that. I always get tricked into letting her move me around our house to wherever she wants to attack me. Sometimes it is on the couch, other times the hammock. She is very good at moving me all over, but I do not mind. I kind of like it, to tell you the truth."

For some people the moving hug can be functional. It gets them to another location while letting them maintain contact with each other. Says one young woman, "It's easy to move during a hug. My hubby and I do it all the time. You shift your body and just walk him toward where you want to end up. It's kind of *I want to do something but I don't want to let go.*"

Mostly, however, this is a playful and fun variation of the basic hug. "I just set our bodies in motion by gently moving myself if we're in a slow, sensual mood," reports a young woman in her early twenties. "If we're being a bit more playful, we just throw each other around—all in fun." Says another woman, "Sometimes I move him around when I'm in a jokey or really happy mood. It shows him how much I'm feeling at the time and also how much I like to tease him."

Other couples like to twirl themselves around during a moving hug. A medical student from Denver writes, "When I'm particularly happy, there tends to be an excess of spinning during hugs. They usually continue until one or both of us (preferably the latter) get dizzy and fall down."

The
$\mathcal{C}$ONTINENTAL HUG

An attractive young woman came up to me after a recent lecture and told me her boyfriend was *nothing* like the men in Europe. Other people were waiting to ask questions, but I wanted to hear what she had to say so I stepped back toward the stage.

"Excuse me?"

She followed me and repeated her comment. "They really know how to kiss and hug in Europe."

"Is that so?"

"Yes!"

"What is it they do differently?"

She blushed and shrugged her shoulders and seemed to shiver almost imperceptibly. Then she inched closer and lowered her voice.

"I was there this summer and met a few guys from France."

"Can you tell me about them?"

"Well, in Paris I lived with a musician for three months while I was studying. At first I thought he had a low sex drive because after our dates he would only hug me, nothing more. He was like a brother to me the first two months. We used to sit with our backs against the wall because he had no furniture—only a piano—and he'd put his arm around me and smoke a cigarette. I always wanted to kiss him and have sex because he was very good-looking and sensitive. But he just hugged me for hours in that bare apartment. Then he'd play the piano and we'd have dinner and go to bed *together* and hug all night."

"Thank you for sharing that with me."

"Why aren't guys in the States like that?"

That's what I'd like to know.

If only we could hug like Europeans! We'd have our lovers getting wistful and nostalgic when they talked about *us*. And the funny thing is that it's not really difficult to hug like Europeans. It takes a little getting used to, maybe a little restraint when it comes to sex, and a small amount of patience. But it's certainly worth learning their style of hugging if you want to be romantic.

Here are the particulars about how they hug in Europe. I hope that from each section you can pick up a few pointers and ideas to incorporate into your own hugging practice.

Belgium

They always hug and kiss in greeting.

Czechoslovakia

A high school girl from the Czech Republic writes: "My boyfriend is very active in the Communist party. He likes to hug with two arms around my arms so I can't move. I was at a meeting with him and noticed the other men hugging the same way, so maybe it's a political style."

Denmark

The Danes hug early in the morning and late at night. They don't hug as much in the afternoon. "We work all day and hug in the early morning and evening," writes a woman from Copenhagen who has two small children. "My husband hugs while he drinks wine and listens to music. Sometimes our little ones climb up onto our laps while we're hugging and they join in the fun."

The Netherlands

Dutch hugs are repetitive. A Canadian who visited the country E-mailed this comment: "I stayed in Holland for a year and it took a while to get used to how compulsive the natives are. They give you one hug, you think it's over. But when you try and pull away they quickly yank you back and give you a second and third in quick succession. I found this pattern of repeated hugs very funny at first. But when I got back to Toronto my family was astonished to find that I was doing it to them!"

England

The greatest difference between English and American hugging styles according to respondents who have experienced both is that the English tend to show less of their emotion in public. This does not mean that they aren't passionate in private.

"I'm glad this is anonymous," says a twenty-seven-year-old from London. "My boyfriend is a little shy. I'm from a very loving family, but he was raised by a rather distant stepmother and a father who was always at work. He took a while to get used to hugging me. But he hugs like a maniac when we're alone together. When I was in the States in my early twenties (I went to college there) I had some American boyfriends who hugged and kissed in public more. But in private the hugs are the same, except that English boys are more polite about the whole experience."

Estonia

The Estonians are crazy huggers in public, they can't get enough. But unlike some other Europeans, they make a point of seeking out only the most beautiful spots to hug in public. "We have no shame here," said one Estonian in his early thirties. "We look for a picturesque street, the little alley overlooking the seashore, a bridge over a river, and then we hug like we were the only two people there."

Finland

The Finnish hug is primarily nonsexual. They like sex, of course, but they can hug for long periods of time without becoming aroused. This is a key point to keep in mind when trying to hug like a European. To hug like a Finn, see how long you can hug without wanting to have sex.

France

"Well, the French are unable to hug someone without a brief kiss on both cheeks," comments one young Finn who's visited Sweden, Norway, Denmark, Germany, and France. "That style may be difficult to adopt for someone not born to a society like France, where it is the default."

It is important to note that the French greeting hug—complete with kisses—is not the same as the French romantic hug.

"I studied in France for a semester during my sophomore year of high school," writes a young woman from Texas. "I had a French boyfriend who was the most exquisite lover you could imagine. He would hug me with his hands always traveling up and down my back, over my arms, nuzzling his face into my hair, my neck, pressing his lips behind my ears and across my cheeks. *Mmmmm!* Hugging was an art form with him. And when we went to dances I noticed that the other kids from France were the same. You could watch them making out in the dark, their hands continuously moving. It was beautiful. Coming back to the States was a letdown."

Germany

Germans are very time-oriented huggers. They want to make sure they hug at precisely the right moment. A Canadian traveling in Berlin E-mailed this account of his experience with a German girl: "It's kind of like one of those scenes out of some mushy romance movie. I saw this girl on the UBahn in Berlin and something must have clicked because the two of us did all sorts of flirty gestures while on the train. When we got off at the station I went up to talk to her. I spoke a dozen words of German (forgetting everything I had learned, as I hadn't had a class in eight years) and she spoke no English. As I said, we just sort of clicked. We 'talked' on the platform at the Anhaulter Bahnhof for about ten or fifteen minutes. Then her train was coming, my train was coming. (And I had to get to the train station to leave for Prague that night. Damn!) It totally slipped my mind to ask her name, take her picture, anything. All I could do was debate in my head whether *schoen* meant 'beautiful' in German and 'clean' in Dutch, or vice versa. So finally I told her she was *schoen* (got it right, lucky me!), I hugged her, and even gave her a little kiss. It was wonderful, even though I don't think she hugged any differently than anyone else I've hugged—except that her timing was unforgettable!"

Hungary

Hungarians are unreserved and warm, and so are their hugs. Says a young man from Chicago, "There's a difference in how they hug in Hungary. Hugs in the States are reserved, hugs in Hungary are much more involved. Specifically, there's a difference in space near the groin area. Americans protect that area too much, causing them to angle themselves while hugging."

Iceland

Icelandic hugs are done with lots of pressing action from both torsos, according to a Londoner who visited his wife's family in Iceland.

Israel

Girls in Israel are passionate and hug in a very exciting way, according to guys who have visited the country. Their hugs often include a subtle wriggling movement of the pelvis and chest. "I was in Israel for a month last year," says a businessman in his early thirties. "At lunchtime we went out to a park, and a woman with big breasts took off her shirt to get some sun. She thought nothing of it. Later when we went back to the office I couldn't stop fantasizing about her. At a party later that week I took the opportunity to hug her and she pressed her chest to mine. While hugging her I kept thinking of what I had seen. During the hug she wriggled left and right, as if to get closer to me. It's a nice effect."

Italy

From a twenty-two-year-old Italian university student: "I dated many Italians before I met my American girlfriend, so I think I can make a comparison. We have two kinds of hugs here: greeting hugs and romantic hugs. Greeting hugs are for friends, lovers, relatives, casual acquaintances. Romantic hugs are different. In America you hug a little, then you stop. Here the hug is part of everything. If we're going for a walk, it's time to hug. If we're driving, we're hugging in the car. At school between classes it's the same, more hugs. Everywhere it's expected. She took a little time getting used to it. She thought I was being too friendly at first, too demanding. Now she's relaxed. She enjoys it. She adapted to our ways. And she's happier."

Norway

Norwegian hugs are powerful and steady. From a fellow who lives in Oslo comes this comment: "If we aren't inclined to hug you, there's no use trying to hug us because our mind is set and we'll stick out our arm and shake your hand instead. But once we decide to hug, we do it with all our heart and soul. We're not a cold people, even though our climate is chilly. The world has the wrong image of us. We're a strong people, and our hugs are more vigorous than those I've received from natives of southern Europe—Portugal, France, Greece, and so on. Even Germans don't hug as strongly as we do. It is comforting to hug a Norwegian. They grip you and you feel reassured. They won't let you go without transferring some of their strength to you through their hug."

Poland

"My boyfriend is a member of Solidarity (the independent labor union) and was a personal aide to Lech Walesa. He told me the way Lech Walesa hugs. He actually saw him hugging like this. He takes the woman in his arms and then reaches out his hands and picks up a big sandwich and eats it while he hugs her. My boyfriend always tells me that he actually saw this, and now he eats his dinner while hugging me. He is always picking things up while hugging me and blaming it on Lech Walesa."

Portugal

The Portuguese hug warmly, like other Europeans, according to respondents from Lisbon, but are more keenly interested in how you are enjoying the hug. After hugging you they will look closely at your face to see if you liked the hug or need another one.

Scotland

One hug, one kiss. That's the norm. They are also fond of hugging with all their clothes on, which is similar to some teenage petting behavior in the United States. The Scots will hug with their clothes on for long periods of time even when they're inside and alone together. They also hug after eating when both partners are quite content and full.

Spain

When you're feeling down or sad about anything, the Spanish will notice it and give you a hug to make you feel better. A young woman from Spain who came to the United States to attend college writes: "I miss the pick-me-up hugs from my family and friends in Madrid. But some students here are from Puerto Rico, and they do the same for me. For example, recently I went to a Spanish Mass at school. All the kids there were from Spain or Puerto Rico or South America, and we had a lot in common. I was feeling blue. I saw my friend Lily, and she gave me a big hug during the part of Mass where you offer a sign of peace. She said she wanted to cheer me up. It was so considerate of her, and it immediately made me feel better. Of course I'll return the favor someday soon if I can."

Sweden

"I was staying with a girl from Lund, Sweden," writes a young man from Canada who was traveling in France. "She always gave me very nice hugs in greeting and departing. The hugs were casual and friendly, nothing romantic to them. She had a boyfriend, and once I saw her hugging him when he came to pick her up for a date. What a difference! She bent one knee while hugging him. Was I ever jealous!"

How to hug like a European

- ☛ Hug after eating.
- ☛ Forget about sex.
- ☛ Add squeezes to your hugs.
- ☛ Hug for longer periods of time.
- ☛ Time your hugs to make the most impact.
- ☛ Keep your hands moving across your partner's back.
- ☛ When traveling, seek out romantic locations to stop and hug.
- ☛ Observe your partner closely during and after a hug to see if they need another.
- ☛ Don't complain. If you're uncomfortable, simply move into a more comfortable position.
- ☛ Move your pelvis closer when you hug. In other words, don't be afraid to touch your legs and groin area to theirs during the hug.
- ☛ Bend a knee, pick up something to eat, move, walk, and do other things while hugging.

Next time you travel to Europe, here are some suggestions for romantic places to hug.

In your opinion, what is the most romantic place to hug in Europe?

"In Venice in a gondola."

"Along the Seine in Paris at sunset."

"Prague. If I *ever* go back to Prague it's going to be with a significant other and we're going to hug *everywhere* in the city. It's the most romantic city I've been to in Europe.

"In train stations of almost any country in Europe."

"In Rome, the city of love, with mad taxis whizzing past in the street and people passing by and smiling at you."

The
SAME-SEX HUG

"One of the things we learned at CIA training school was how to hug in foreign countries," wrote a fellow in his early fifties. "Our purpose was to avoid suspicion and blend in with the local culture. So we had to know how to hug members of the same sex in foreign countries. In Europe it's expected that you'll hug other men. They taught us how to do it at Camp Peary, a secret compound near Williamsburg, Virginia. We'd go out in the field and hug guys in the class like they do in Europe. It was the oddest part of my training. I'm retired now, but I'm still a great hugger!"

You don't have to be a CIA operations officer to hug members of the same sex. People do it all the time even here in the United States.

Hugging members of the same sex is different from hugging romantically in several important ways. Same-sex hugs are shorter and less intimate. They mostly occur in greeting and leaving rather than as an ongoing part of the interaction between companions. People typically talk during these hugs, saying things such as "Hello" or "See you soon." And finally, the architecture of the hug is different. Usually same-sex hugs involve putting your arms around your friend up near the shoulders. Your feet will be further apart than in romantic hugs, and your legs and groin areas don't touch.

Do you ever hug friends of the same sex? What is this like?

WOMEN:
"It makes me happy that they're my friends. These hugs are occasionally longer than hugs with family members and guys. Sometimes I talk if I'm excited or if I'm trying to soothe somebody."

"It feels weird to encounter breasts. It's different from a romantic hug because you don't necessarily share emotions, and the sexual attraction isn't there. The hug just says that you're my friend and I like you."

"There's the same amount of body contact, but there's more conversation."

MEN:
"During these hugs you know there won't be any touchy-feely stuff. I wonder sometimes if people think we're gay, but I let them think what they will. I've had a few intimate hugs from male friends. Less body contact. No talking."

"Most of my close male friends are open with them, actually. I will admit that there is some effort to insure that they're not romantic. I've noticed that hugs with pats on backs seem to be 'I care about you, but be assured I don't have designs on your body' hugs."

"Some of my same-sex friends give me short, terse, silent hugs that end quickly. It seems there is some fear or some taboo (for them) that is associated with a same-sex hug. But I am fortunate to have friends who don't give a damn about those taboos and exchange full-blown hugs with impunity, same-sex or not."

Business hugs

Only one-half of 1 percent of respondents ever hugged in a business context. While kissing is acceptable in some business situations (see *The Art of Kissing* for more on this), hugging almost never is. Said one young man, "The town I'm working in now is small and has more homophobes on average than Honolulu. So I don't hug business associates as much as I used to, let alone coworkers. I personally like these hugs even though they're formal. Hugging in suits always made me feel like an extra in a *Godfather* movie."

Sports hugs

A specialized version on the same-sex hug is the hug you get when you're an amateur or professional athlete. Usually these hugs occur at an emotional moment, just before an important contest, or after a victory. Jake LaMotta always used to kiss the fighters he defeated in the ring. There was no suggestion of homosexuality. In his view, he simply wanted to show that it was all just a game.

Sports hugs are usually brief and involve the upper body only. You can see them on television during football games. It seems that the more violent the sport, the more it justifies these expressions of physical contact. In some ways it acts as a counterweight to the violence of the sport itself.

The

ℬED HUG

"One night I found Michelle in bed with another man."
Jack was on the phone talking to me about his wife.

"What did you do?"

"Nothing."

"Weren't you furious?"

"Well, they denied that they had slept together. And this
was before I married her."

"Who was the guy?"

"It was Frank. I came home late from work and they
were both passed out. Michelle was on her side, completely
naked. There was an empty bottle of wine on the floor.
Frank had on just his boxer shorts and was sleeping next to
her."

"So how could you react so calmly?"

"Well, like I said, I questioned them about it and they
both denied everything. So I never knew for sure."

"It certainly sounds suspicious to me, Jack!"

"I know, but the funny thing was that Frank didn't seem
like a real threat to me."

"What makes you say that? I mean after all, he was sleeping in the same bed with her!"

"Well, he had his back to her and was curled up in a fetal

position. She was completely naked, but she also had her back toward him. And they were about three feet apart in that small bed I used to have. You know, it was actually the position of their bodies that made me feel relieved. They didn't *look* like lovers."

Jack's analysis of his wife's sleeping position with Frank is right on target according to research conducted by bedroom analyst Samuel Dunkell, M.D. There is a lot you can learn about a couple by the way they sleep and hug together in bed. In his book *Sleep Positions: The Night Language of the Body* (New York: Morrow, 1977) Dunkell suggests that couples who sleep back-to-back are usually further apart psychologically than couples who sleep in more interactive positions. "The way we sleep is the way we live," says Dunkell. So maybe Jack was right not to worry about a man who slept back-to-back with his wife.

In an effort to examine hugging and sleep positions in the bedroom, I asked whether couples ever went to bed for the express purpose of just hugging while lying down (not sleeping and not having sex). It turns out that hugging in bed is quite a popular activity. Survey results indicate that 74 percent of women and 62 percent of men sometimes get into bed just to hug. When we examine only those couples that enjoyed a close and affectionate relationship, this percentage jumps to 94 percent. In other words, the closer a couple feels and the happier they rate their relationship, the more likely they are to hug in bed. Couples that enjoy a good relationship tend to hug in bed more than couples that are experiencing difficulties.

"Yes, we do go to bed just to hug," says a thirty-year-old woman from northern California. "My husband and I both like it because when we do this we aren't distracted by things around us and we can focus just on each other. We do it every couple of months and should probably do it more, but time runs out in the day."

A young man who just got engaged and who is admittedly in a terrific relationship says, "We somehow ended up with a pattern. Come home from school, change into shorts and ratty shirts, lie on the bed and hug for about an hour just talking or resting. Then we watch reruns of *The Simpsons*. We do it every weekday. It's our special downtime. Sometimes we're so busy that it's the only time and way we have to share and be intimate. Usually we lie facing each other, our arms and legs draped over one another."

In 79 percent of cases a hug in bed can make one or both members of a couple fall asleep. Paradoxically, hugging in bed can also have an opposite effect. Sometimes it can lead to excitement and arousal. A woman executive reports that hugging in bed often leads to sex. But this paradox can perhaps be explained. Alex Comfort in *The Joy of Sex* (New York: Pocket, 1974) points out that sex includes things other than intercourse. One of the things he classifies as sex is simply resting together. Which may explain why close to 30 percent of our sample reported that hugging in bed often led to sexual excitement.

Ironically, this sexual excitement can sometimes break the mood for the partner who just wanted to hug affectionately and nonsexually in bed. A young woman commented, "The only thing I don't like about hugging in bed is when my focus is one place and he wants it to turn into sex or vice versa."

Finding the right position

Hugging in bed can be bliss or it can be torture. It all depends on how you position your bodies and how tolerant you are. You may have to go through some contortions before you find a comfortable spot for your arms and legs. One position many couples like is face-to-face, each lying on his or her side. About 40 percent also like it when the woman lies on her back and the man lies next to her and hugs her from the side or vice versa.

The spoon position is by far the most popular bedroom hugging style. Almost 72 percent of men and women rely on it regularly. It is a position some lovers come back to now and then throughout the night. It gets its name from the fact that you lie with your front to your partner's back, nestled together like two spoons. One young man describes his reliance on this classic position:"Usually we start facing each other, then after we doze we end up spooning with her in front. In the middle of the night, my lover sometimes sits up and sleeps like that—leaving me just to curl up around her back and hug her that way. We wake up every morning back in the spoon position." And a young woman says,"Falling asleep embraced, any way, is the best. Spoon-style, with him behind me, is my favorite."

Some people spoon to keep warm at night. "If it's cold I like to fall asleep hugging to get warm and stay warm," says one young woman. "If it's really cold we sleep like spoons or back-to-back for warmth and just to know the other person is there."

Couples often change position several times during the night. There is nothing abnormal about this. In fact, it might be abnormal if you *didn't* change position. Says one young woman, "Generally we begin face-to-face, each curled in the fetal position. Then we move to our sides, either spooning each other with one of our fronts to the other's back or butt-to-butt in the fetal position. And then always I move to my stomach and turn my head to the side opposite him."

A surprisingly large number of people don't like hugging when sleeping in the same bed with a lover. About 8 percent say they can't fall asleep if someone is hugging them. For example, a thirty-year-old single male says, "I can never quite get to sleep while someone is hugging me, even if it's just an arm or head lightly pressed against mine."

Nearly 40 percent of respondents occasionally need time off during at least part of the night so they can sleep alone. To the partner who doesn't need space, this can feel like rejection. But remember that not everyone has the same tolerance for physical contact. For example, one young woman who is very strong reports that her boyfriend is more delicate and she resents this: "He is especially eggshell-like and has *no* tolerance for pressure or pain to the skin. For this I fault him and wish he was more manly." Some people need to be by themselves so much they even tell their partner to move over or push them away during the night. If your partner does this, don't take it personally—it may be that they just have a greater need for personal space while sleeping.

During the night, do you ever need time off from contact with your partner while sleeping? If so, why? How do you get the space you need? Does your lover ever resent your need for space?

WOMEN:
"Yes, I need to sleep contact free. I move around a lot. My partner doesn't actually resent it, but I'm sure he would love it if I'd sleep entwined with him."

"Yes, I do need my own space and get that by shifting over to the edge of the bed, and if that isn't enough I ask my husband to scoot over a little. I often need space to be comfortable. Sometimes you can't sleep because you feel like you can't breathe or you get too hot or the blankets get too tangled."

"Yes, I do. I need to change positions or I'm too hot. I roll away from him to get space or I push him gently away. Yes, he often resents this."

"We sometimes need space from one another during the night, but when we move apart it's not problematic. We just do it but we make sure that some part of our bodies, no matter how slight, is touching at all times. If we wake up in the middle of the night to find we aren't touching, we rectify the situation immediately. This is one aspect of our relationship behind closed doors that is critical to our success as lovers."

MEN:
"I've learned to sleep alone. Even if it's a gentle hug, I can't sleep. If my girlfriend is hugging or touching me I think about her. It keeps me awake. I just ask her for some space. She also needs space to fall asleep, though she *can* fall asleep while hugging me."

"No, but I suppose subconsciously *she* does. She's more apt to move during the night (or even kick!). It doesn't bother me."

"After prolonged contact it feels good to get back into your own space for a while. Nothing offensive is implied or inferred, and some casual contact is usually resumed in a moment."

The

ℊ ROUP HUG

Amy and her boyfriend Kevin are preparing to leave a party. Their host, Sally, a big bossy type, has been dating a guy from France for several months. Everyone's had a few too many. Sally comes over to Amy and Kevin, Frenchman in tow, holding hands.

"Let's hug," she says.

Amy at first cringes. But she soon gets used to the fact that she's in a four-way hug. The group makes a small circle. Everyone has his or her arms around two other people. It's a little like a football huddle, only it's more familiar and friendly. You can smell the beer on the Frenchman's breath. A few words are spoken as the hug continues. Then after about a minute it breaks up.

Amy feels that she's part of a circle of close friends—even though she just met the Frenchman tonight and will probably never see him again, knowing Sally's penchant for changing partners every few months.

Earlier in the week, Amy and two surgeons had hugged in the operating room after reattaching the ear of a patient who tore it almost all the way off in a bicycle accident. Teamwork. That's the idea behind the group hug. But that's not all. It's also a social hug. You see it in sports circles and other nonbusiness situations. It can even be done with large groups of ten or more.

Often this hug is accomplished when one person specifically suggests the idea.

"I've experienced group hugs many times," says a young man from Hawaii. "Me and a female coworker at a newspaper I worked at a couple of years ago tried to counteract low morale with the *Ka Leo* Hug Therapy Program. (*Ka Leo* was the name of the paper.) Every member of the staff was encouraged to have a hug, preferably from her or myself—the professional huggers. For particularly cranky staff members, hugs were mandatory. Led to some pretty interesting days in the office. Three-way hugs were usually initiated by a practicing member of the Hug Therapy Program and were started with the battle cry 'Group hug!' Pretty simple. They last longer, they're a lot more entertaining, and they make you feel . . . well, good. Like you belong to a cohesive group."

Sometimes a group hug just happens by itself without direction from anyone, the natural by-product of being together with people you like.

"At gatherings of close friends, we often have spur-of-the-moment mass hugs," explained one engineer. "Nobody in particular initiates them. They last about a minute, and they're warm and comforting."

Keep in mind that sometimes a group hug won't give you as much satisfaction as a two-person hug. You may even experience some feelings of jealousy during them, as this young woman explains: "I have experienced quite a few three-way hugs. During a bonding exercise in drama class we had to go around and tell people nonverbally how we felt about the final performance. 'Nonverbally' generally equals 'hugging,' so that's what everyone does. Joe, my friend who was going to move far away soon, was in front of me, so I touched him lightly for him to turn around and

I hugged him for a while. I don't quite remember who joined us, but it was one of our mutual friends. It was fairly long, lasting until the end of the exercise a few moments later. I'd like to say it was nice, but I actually felt kind of jealous sharing my hug with Joe with another person."

Three-way hugs with a child

Three-way hugs are ideal for times when a couple of adults are with a child. You simply lift the youngster and sandwich him or her between the two of you. The child should be encouraged to hug one adult. The second adult presses her stomach against the child's back and puts her arms around the first adult. If the child can stand, you do the same thing, only you don't have to lift him up. A hug like this fosters closeness and makes everyone—even the kid who's being squished—feel connected despite differences in body size.

PART THREE

Hugging Technique

ℋUGGING

TECHNIQUE

"You don't like to hug!"

He couldn't believe his ears.

How could she accuse him of *not* liking to hug? How in heaven could she think he *didn't* like feeling her body pressed to his? He loved it! Was she for real?

"You don't like to hug!"

But she kept saying it!

Didn't she know he loved getting his hands on her?

The truth is he liked *sexual* contact. Most men like sexual contact. But when it comes to nonsexual contact the majority of guys don't see the sense in giving their partner a romantic embrace containing only a very *low* level of sexual energy. The kind of energy that will make her heat up . . . eventually.

What they don't have is good hugging technique.

This section will give it to you.

Our discussion of technique is geared to help you achieve the right balance between romance and sex. Sometimes it's better to let sex fade into the background while you concentrate on loving and letting your hearts beat as one. Before you know it you'll be hugging for the sake of hugging.

And your lover will be getting more turned on than you expect.

What is the best overall position for hugging?

The consensus is that when standing the best position for hugging is your basic front-to-front hug. Never neglect this classic. Let all your forays into the realm of strange and creative hugs come back to it eventually. It is done heart-to-heart, cheek-to-cheek, with your arms around each other and your legs and hips touching. As one young man says, "I guess the best hug is the simplest. Front-to-front, arms around each other, and (if applicable) lips-to-lips, too!"

Add a little passion to this one by following the European custom of pressing your groin area into your partner's during the hug. This isn't necessarily sexual contact. It's simply a greater physical connection than is usual in the United States. In other words, don't be shy about body contact during this hug.

Do women worry about touching their breasts against men who aren't their lover during a hug?

Thirty percent of women occasionally worry about this, usually because they don't want their hugs to be taken as sexual come-ons. Said one married woman in her midtwenties, "I don't want my hugs to be misinterpreted by the hugee or by my husband, who may be present and watching." For most women, this was more of a problem when they were adolescents. "When I was going through puberty I worried about it, but no longer," says one woman in her thirties.

Instead of worrying about this, some women actually get a secret thrill from the idea. They may even want the guy to enjoy it. A woman from New Zealand said, "Depends on who the man is! I worry about it if I'm not attracted to him, but if I am, then hey, I will enjoy it and hope that he does too."

Others realize that men may get a little charge out of coming into contact with their bosom, but it doesn't bother the woman. A thirty-year-old married woman put it this way: "No, I don't really worry about my breasts touching men who aren't my lover when hugging. I figure there is no choice when I hug them, the breasts are there. So it gives them a little thrill maybe, but that's all they get."

One sixteen-year-old said boldly: "No, I usually try to!"

What are the hugging secrets of the Orient?

The first secret of Oriental hugging is to do it in a secluded spot where you can be alone with your lover. Responses from Korea, China, Japan, and Taiwan reveal that public hugs are not very popular there. Instead, all their hugging energy gets released when the lovers are in private. Then their hugs are even more romantic than Western hugs.

Another Oriental hugging technique involves static hugs. These are hugs in which both partners lock their arms around each other and hold on tightly for a minute or more, not moving, but straining every muscle in their body. "The amount of energy released in a static hug is tremendous," reports a young man from southern China. "I experienced this when I was seven years old with the woman who is to be my wife. It is also a very erotic hug when you pass puberty. When done properly, it expresses your deep love in a nonsexual way. It is a chaste hug because you don't move. And it is based on the yoga principle of kundalini energy."

For more secrets of Oriental hugging, dip into the *Kama Sutra*, a first-century book of advice for both young and experienced lovers by the Indian sage Vatsyayana. You'll discover plenty of romantic ideas, such as:

- ☛ **The rubbing hug.** You walk slowly together with your lover, either in the dark or in an outdoor mall or in a lonely place, and rub your bodies against each other.
- ☛ **The pressing hug.** After doing a rubbing hug as described above, one of the lovers presses the other's body forcibly against a wall or pillar.
- ☛ **The piercing hug.** The woman "in a lonely place bends down, as if to pick up something, and pierces, as it were, a man sitting or standing, with her breasts, and the man in return takes hold of them."
- ☛ **The climbing-of-a-tree hug.** The woman, having placed one of her feet on the foot of her lover, and the other on one of his thighs, passes one of her arms around his back and places the other on his shoulders. Then she makes low sounds of singing and cooing and acts like she wants to climb up him in order to have a kiss.

Is it a good idea to hug and talk?

Most people seem to think so. In fact, talking while hugging is even more popular than talking while kissing. Survey results indicate that 78 percent of men and 85 percent of women occasionally talk during a hug.

"While hugging, we tell each other how comfortable we are," says one woman, "and how good we smell, look, feel."

If you're greeting a friend, the best way to do it is to continue your conversation without interruption while you throw your arms around the person for a quick greeting hug. Talking even eases your transition into and out of a hug. The basic technique is described by a fellow in his early twenties: "Sometimes I barely break the conversation when giving a hug. While hugging my love, of course, I say 'I love you.' Either that or I nibble her neck or ear, which is more fun but potentially dangerous."

Can lovers hug over the phone?

Yes, and they enjoy doing it, too. In response to survey questions, 43 percent of men and 56 percent of women report they hug over the phone.

There are two ways to do this. One, you just say "hug" to your lover. The other way to give a phone hug is to describe to your lover just how you will hug him or her when you next meet. You could also pretend you're giving the hug in real time right over the phone. You and the recipient obviously have to use a little imagination for this to work.

Hugging tip

You can also include hugs in love letters. They usually appear under the signature as a line of *XOXO*'s where each *X* stands for a kiss and each *O* for a hug.

What's the best way to greet someone with a hug?

Approach the other person slowly so that you can see what kind of mood they're in. Smile and say a few complimentary words, such as "Good to see you." Give them a quick embrace while you continue talking. If the person is a close friend or family member, a single air kiss on the side of the cheek is optional. This air kiss usually doesn't involve contact between your lips and their cheek, instead you just kiss the air to the side of their face.

Greeting hugs are usually shorter than romantic hugs. According to one young woman, "Generally if I haven't seen someone I care about for a while, I will hug them hello. The hugs are usually tight but quick, not at all sexual (unless I am hugging my fiancé)." But more intense hugs are common after prolonged periods of separation. As one woman explains, "After a lengthy separation the hugs are longer and more emotional—we cling more."

Most people greet long-lost friends with a hug that expresses their joy at being reunited. Says one woman, "If I haven't seen someone in a long time, the first thing I like to do is give them a really big hug that tells them how much they were missed." According to another woman, "The long separation hug feels like a relief especially when I haven't hugged someone for a while."

Why do some people refuse to hug?

About 22 percent of the population never hugs. They usually are too shy or too unsure of themselves to hug. Often these people have received little affection in their lives or are uncomfortable with their bodies.

Huggers have various ways of dealing with nonhuggers. Probably the best way is simply to accept and respect nonhuggers. "It sort of makes you feel rejected when you encounter a person who refuses to hug," says a married woman from Nebraska. "But you have to remember not to take it personally and abide by their wishes and not hug them."

Some people react rather strongly when people refuse to hug them. An affectionate fifteen-year-old says, "I *hate* it when people blatantly refuse to be hugged. I end up being less emotionally close to those people than to more affectionate people. Maybe it makes them feel better, but it makes me feel hostile and offended."

What's the best way to hug in a car?

Park and hug. This is the method recommended by the National Highway Traffic Safety Administration because it's safer than hugging while driving.

Statistics from around the world indicate that three out of four people like to hug in a car. One young man from North Carolina likes it because "there's a mystique about parking and doing sexy things in cars, for example at Lookout Point."

If the car is in motion and you're both in front, the best idea is to have the passenger hug the driver—not the other way around. Says a man in his midthirties from Ohio, "My girlfriend hugs me. I don't while driving because I don't want to crash." The passenger has greater freedom to move and control the hug, so this method is safest.

"If my girl is seated beside me, she turns toward me and leans over to deliver the hug," reports a young man from Reims, France. "If she's in back she just hugs me with her arms around the seat. People drive so crazy in this city we have to be very careful when we hug."

Is there any value in hugging pets?

According to recent research, hugging pets can lower your blood pressure and make you more relaxed. If you're elderly, hugging a pet can increase your life expectancy and offer significant protection against stroke and heart failure.

About 30 percent of people have pets and of that number about 95 percent like to hug their pets. Dogs are the most popular and huggable animal.

Cats are trickier.

"I can't hug my cat; she would scratch me," writes a woman from Indonesia.

"I have a cat who I like to pick up and hug," says a fifteen-year-old girl from Montana. "I really love her, but she doesn't like to be held. When I'm holding her and she wants to get down, I feel disappointed and even rejected! Just by a cat! But when she lets me hug her and starts purring because she likes it, it gives me such a feeling of— not accomplishment, but like I did something right and someone else appreciates it."

Tips for hugging cats

- ☛ Don't do it very often.
- ☛ It really helps if you clip their claws!
- ☛ Don't hug them for too long.
- ☛ Don't hug them too tight all the time, or they'll hate you. If you do it softly and gently they'll like that much better.
- ☛ Remember that you can hug cats only when they want to be hugged, just like people.

How do you hug a baby?

Actually, you don't usually hug babies, you cuddle them. When hugging, you put your arms or hands around a person and apply some pressure. When cuddling, you are more tender and may even hold the infant in your arms or hands. You can hold a baby to your chest to comfort it, or you can rock it back and forth in your arms. Many people like to hold a baby up to their cheek.

"Holding them in my arms, I bring them close to me and often put my cheek on their head," says a twenty-three-year-old from Canada.

You have to be forgiving when you cuddle babies. They may not appreciate it. When they're in the mood for it, however, it can be fun for both you and the infant. Says one young man, "Usually I just raise 'em and press them against my cheek. It's best when they're not wearing shirts—then you can follow up with a tummy fart."

How do you hug a teddy bear?

You can hug a teddy bear tight and squeeze it with all your strength. It will never complain. Most people hugged stuffed animals when they were children, and some continue the practice into adulthood, often just before sleep or when they need emotional comfort and there is no human around. A woman in her late twenties who had been sexually abused as a teenager keeps a collection of stuffed animals in her bedroom. She hugs them each night because it makes her feel secure.

Sometimes hugging a teddy bear can make you feel sorry for yourself, as one young woman reports: "Yes, it's comforting, but I also think it can make you feel self-pitying—*Oh, I've got no-one to hug. I'll just sit here and hug my teddy bear.*" There's certainly something about teddy bears that seems to evoke feelings. Says one thirty-four-year-old woman from Ohio, "Sometimes when I feel sad I drag out my old teddy bear and hold it. It helps me release some of my emotions."

"I always hug my stuffed elephant while I go to sleep," says a nineteen-year-old woman. "It's a ritual I've followed every night, with the exception of a few, since I was old enough to hug him. He's very small, but it's comforting to know that *something* is receiving your affection, even if it's not another person."

How do you hug a pillow?

Forty percent of men and 63 percent of women sometimes hug their pillows. Some hug a pillow as a substitute for their childhood stuffed animal.

"It makes you feel more mature because the pillow doesn't have big eyes and ears, but it can be just as soft if not softer and almost as comforting," says a woman from Utah.

Twenty percent of people also mentioned that a pillow gives them some comfort when they're missing someone. Says one young architectural student, "I've hugged a pillow when sad and lonely or upset." And another woman notes, "I sleep with a body pillow because my husband works during the time I sleep. Since I'm used to having him to lean into, the pillow in a way feels like leaning into someone."

When is the best time to hug on a date?

Without doubt the best time to hug is at the *end* of a date. Most people hug either at the beginning of a date when they're saying hello or at the end when saying good night. Of these two options, the good-night hug is by far the more popular and emotionally satisfying. If a couple knows each other well, of course, hugs during a date are always welcome.

"A good date needs a hug to close properly," says a male

college student. "If there was a lot of emotional bonding and personal sharing, I would feel inclined to acknowledge our sincerity in being with each other with a hug. In short, always hug to close a date. But if you can also get hugs throughout, go for it!"

If you create a romantic atmosphere during a date, hugs are more likely at the end. "Good conversation will make things romantic," says one man from Pittsburgh. "Then you can hug when you say good night."

Do lovers like to hug when high?

More than 92 percent of men and women prefer to hug while sober. Says one woman, "I prefer hugging sober because the hugs are more coordinated. Also, if the person is drunk, they might throw up on you." A man from Atlanta agrees: "Not only do I not drink, I like sober huggers more than drunken ones. There's more of the real person coming out of a sober hug than whatever is coming out of the hug from one is who is in a drunken stupor."

Only about 12 percent of women and 7 percent of men say they like to hug while high on marijuana. Somehow it heightens their sensations, according to those who have tried it.

What should you do with your hands while hugging?

The best thing is to hold your partner's back, then rub up and down gently. Occasionally you may want to grab your partner's buttocks. While this isn't always appreciated (see the section on "What do women expect from men during a hug?" in the chapter "Sex Differences in Hugging"), sometimes your partner will love it. Just be sensitive to his or her wishes. Whatever you do during a hug, don't let your hands go dead. Says one woman, "Don't hesitate to let those hands roam! When we hug my hands are either rubbing my boyfriend's back or feeling his butt. I like him to do the same with me."

What to do with your hands during a hug

- ☞ Wrap them around his neck or shoulders.
- ☞ Rub his back gently from the shoulders down.
- ☞ Rest them in the small of his back.
- ☞ Squeeze his back.
- ☞ Lightly pat his back.
- ☞ Feel his butt.
- ☞ Rest your open palms on his butt.
- ☞ Put them in his back pockets.

The
$\mathcal{A}$RT OF HUGGING

Anyone can put his or her arms around another person and squeeze. But not everyone can communicate excitement and passion through a hug. When all's said and done, the difference between a good hug and a great one is a combination of passion and technique. The techniques in this book are meant to enhance your natural ability and liberate your passion.

My friend Laura was returning home from a year studying in Germany. She had fallen in love with a boy there and was saying good-bye to him. They swore they would meet sometime in the future, but in her heart she knew it was over and they would never see each other again.

"I told him good-bye with a hug and with tears. That hug lasted five full minutes as we waited for my train to pull into the station."

"Couldn't you say anything?"

"No, my voice was gone. I had a lump in my throat and I was crying. I loved him so much I could only hug him good-bye. I gave him something of myself with that hug. Ten years later I can still feel that hug in my heart, and sometimes it still hurts."

If you love someone, love hugging them. When they

hurt, when you hurt, when you're saying hello, when you're saying good-bye, when you're congratulating them, when they're congratulating you—put your arms around them and give something of yourself. Hugs can bridge the gap and heal the wounds that invariably occur in relationships. Hugs are often much better than words at doing this. The point is that hugs will keep you and your lover together emotionally no matter that oceans separate you physically. If you hug sincerely you will get back something that this book could not address at all because it cannot be put into words. When you have mastered the art of hugging, you'll know what that is.

$\mathcal{I}$NDEX

Page numbers in **bold** type indicate primary references.

About the Author

William Cane is the pen name of Michael Christian. His books *The Art of Kissing* and *The Book of Kisses* have been translated into nineteen foreign languages. He has appeared on more than one hundred television and radio programs, including *Today* and *Donahue*. His research has been featured in print and electronic media internationally and has appeared in such newspapers and magazines as *Glamour, Seventeen, Self, Elle,* the *Washington Post,* and the *Chicago Tribune.*

Mr. Cane grew up in New York City, received a law degree from Boston College Law School, and now lives in Brookline, Massachusetts. He practiced law briefly and then turned to teaching, receiving an M.A. in English from Boston University in 1989. He currently teaches English at Boston College and lectures at colleges and universities on the subjects of kissing and hugging.

You can visit Mr. Cane's *The Art of Kissing* homepage on the World-Wide Web at http://ww.acw.com./aok.html and fill out surveys on kissing and hugging and contribute to his next book on relationships.

Author's Note

You can help with my *next* research project by buying this book. The small amount of money I make from it will go toward research I'm currently conducting on the art of romance. If you'd like to receive a questionnaire for that book, please E-mail me at christim@bc.edu or send a stamped self-addressed business-size envelope to P.O. Box 1422, Brookline, MA 02146-0011. When writing from a foreign country, please include a couple of international reply coupons. For information about my lectures on the art of kissing and hugging, contact The Contemporary Issues Agency in Waunakee, Wisconsin: telephone (608) 849-6558.

DON'T MISS

The Art of Kissing
(completely revised and updated edition)

This revised edition of an international classic (now published in eighteen countries and seventeen languages) shares the insights of thousands of kissing connoisseurs from around the world.

The Book of Kisses

More than 500 of the most passionate, romantic, outlandish, and wonderful quotations on the intimate art of kissing.

These books are available at your local bookstore, or use this page for ordering. Send to: Publishers Book & Audio, P.O. Box 120159, Staten Island, NY 10312. Send check or money order—no cash or CODs please. Prices and availability subject to change without notice. Please allow four to six weeks for delivery.

Please send me _____ copies of *The Art of Kissing* and/or _____ copies of *The Book of Kisses* ($6.95 each plus $2.50 shipping and handling). Enclosed is $ _____ .

Name (please print): _____

Address: _____

City/State: _____ Zip: _____